Nicholas Whittaker is the
The Trainspotter as Twentie
written for a wide numbe
Company to the *Sunday Times, and lives with his*
family in north London.

BLUE PERIOD

Notes from a Life in the Titillation Trade

Nicholas Whittaker

VICTOR GOLLANCZ
LONDON

First published in Great Britain 1997
by Victor Gollancz
An imprint of the Cassell Group
Wellington House, 125 Strand, London WC2R 0BB

A Gollancz Paperback Original

A catalogue record for this book is
available from the British Library.

ISBN 0 575 06388 2

Typeset in Great Britain by Rowland Phototypesetting Ltd,
Bury St Edmunds, Suffolk
Printed and bound in Guernsey by
The Guernsey Press Co Ltd, Guernsey, Channel Isles

97 98 99   5 4 3 2 1

Contents

For Deborah Haywood, for being brave enough (or reckless enough) to want such a risqué book dedicated to her when others blanched at the idea; and for all those who still toil in the titillation trade and take more than a fair share of the blame.

1 First Impressions

The switchboard girl looks at the phone in her hand as if it's suddenly turned into a freshly extruded turd.

'Just go and wank yourself . . .' Creep! Shit! Weirdo! She racks her brain for the killer noun. '. . . you fat wanker.'

I'm shocked. It's not that I haven't heard the W-word countless times before. I've done my time in the schoolyard, worked in factories, hung around in pubs. It's hardly shocking, even from women. I've heard it on the lips of schoolgirls, shopgirls, actresses, even nurses, coloured by all kind of accents – wankah, wenker, winker, one cur, vanka. Still, for all that, I've never before heard it uttered with such ball-shrivelling venom.

She slams down the phone so hard that its electrical bits fizz in protest and all the little lights on the switchboard twinkle simultaneously.

'Anus-faced anonymous bastard.'

She looks across at me through the glass hatchway of her cubby-hole. As the nearest male I can't help feeling guilty. I bury my nose in the coverless *Punch* I've picked off the coffee table. Anything to dodge eye-contact.

I'm waiting for a job interview: Assistant Editor on *Fiesta*, Britain's bestselling girlie mag. Ten minutes ago, when I arrived at Galaxy Publications' headquarters in Kilburn, north London, I was puffed up with goofy optimism. Spring syndrome. Even the glummest of us can catch it, charmed by the blue skies, pink blossom, roadsweepers whistling a medley of hits. But watching this girl on the switchboard brings me back to earth. Just what kind of place is this where callers are addressed in such a rough and foul-mouthed fashion? What the hell am I letting myseif in for?

The phone trills again. The girl – Janice I heard someone call her – snatches it up, lips already puckered with disgust, as if she's been picked out of a line-up for compulsory fellation on the cheesey big toe of some old wino. There's none of that customer-care bollocks here. No 'Galaxy. Janice speaking. How may I help you?' Just a curt 'Galaxy'. Nothing else. The tone makes it clear enough, a 'get lost' inflexion that would work equally well in Swahili, Portuguese or old Cornish.

'Do I what?' she demands. 'Frilly what?'

She stares across at me. I tut, I shake my head, I do a tight-lipped 'whatever next?' smile – I'm desperate to show some sympathy. Funny, though, how thoughts get triggered. What kind of knickers *is* she wearing? Sensible white from Marks and Spencer?; girlie pink with teensy blue cornflowers sewn on the waistband?; or the kind they sell at Southend and Margate, with a picture of a smiling snake wriggling through the hole in a doughnut?

Is it too obvious a truism, that you can tell a lot about a girl by the undies she wears? In my own experience any sauciness is always in inverse proportion to the wearer's intentions. Modest knickers, like the quiet girls who wear them, often hold a promise of unexpected pleasures.

I'm worried. Ten minutes ago I was strolling along humming 'What A Wonderful World'; now I'm peering over a magazine trying to picture the knickers of a girl I don't even know. I'm turning into a pervert already. I don't dare look again: with a job like hers Janice has certainly developed some kind of specialized ESP for sussing out men with impure thoughts.

'Tie a knot in your dick. If it's long enough. What do you mean "what"? I said tie a knot in it, you deaf old fart!'

Who can blame her? This isn't any old switchboard she's in charge of: it's a hot-line to a world of wankers, nutters and weirdos. Hieronymous Bosch didn't do switchboards, but if he had this is the one he'd have put in those paintings of hell, a magical box out of which came forth the babble of a million sinners. Any punter who feels like a laugh or a desperate wank can get hold of *Fiesta*'s phone number and ring up. Fair game, aren't they? People who produce dirty magazines can hardly complain about getting dirty phone calls. They deserve all they get.

A tough challenge, but Janice is up to it. In her white blouse and silver crucifix she looks harmlessly demure. It's only when her mouth snaps into action that the illusion shatters. She has lovely teeth: small, white, perfectly aligned. Yet somehow frightening. If her callers are hoping for a thrill they'd stand more chance dipping their lonesome penises in a bucket with a circling piranha.

'Know what I'd do with 'em?' she asks me.

I shake my head. I don't dare imagine. The last thing I want is to be press-ganged into her lynch mob. Janice just smiles, inserts her pencil in the desk-mounted sharpener and whirrs the handle round. She has such lovely lips, but how I hate to see them twisted with this smile, the smile of a medieval torturer, a keeper of racks and thumbscrews. Wood-shavings, mutilated foreskins, it's all the same to her.

Behind me, a wire-glassed security door leads into the main part of the office. Janice exercises control by use of a button on her desk. Some of the staff have it timed to perfection: just as their fingers touch the handle, the lock gives a farty buzz and they sashay through in one smooth, perfectly choreographed sequence.

Others aren't so lucky. This guy in the pink shirt, for instance. Whether he's upset Janice somehow, I don't know, but she seems set upon making life difficult for him. She pretends to be busy, but I can see her smirk, as crafty as a prowling cat after a sparrow. He grabs at the door, pulls hard and, yanked forward by the cruel inevitability of his own inertia, thumps his nose against the glass.

'Prat!'

Janice cackles to herself. She's cheered up noticeably.

Such cruel little amusements obviously help to lighten her day.

I bend cautiously to help him pick up the dropped pile of envelopes. I'm worried about my trousers: I've put a bit of weight on my normally trim backside ('Best Bum in NW3' I was once voted by the girls in the pub where I worked) and my one and only suit doesn't like it. The last thing I want is to split my seams for Janice's amusement.

The man in the pink shirt (the managing director, as I found out later) nods his thanks and goes about his business, pausing only to give Janice a dirty look. She smirks, seemingly protected by a force field of arrogance.

I sit down again, but I can't help wondering why they need a security door anyway. What kind of nutters are on the loose hereabouts?

I'd been out of work for months, supplementing my dole with cash-in-hand bar work at the Belsize Tavern. I loved it. The job included (unofficially) free beer and food and was a neat way of having a good night out. My dole and my pub money combined to make a respectable income, more than enough to fund the illusion of a fast lifestyle. Taking girls out for slap-up meals was no problem.

But the British have a bad attitude to people who serve, making all kinds of crass assumptions about class, wealth and IQ. There'd always be at least one per day. I kept promising myself that the next time anyone snapped their fingers at me because I'd forgotten the lemon slice in their G & T I'd jump across the bar and nut them.

The big Three-O loomed. As much as I enjoyed working in the pub I hankered for a proper job. One with decent wages and a pension and a chance to use my talents – not one where I got home at half-past midnight, too tired to wash and waking next morning smelling of fag smoke and stale beer.

My chance came one Monday morning as, over tea and toast, I made my regular trawl through the media jobs in the *Guardian*. Lacking the qualifications to stroll in and the confidence to bullshit and gatecrash the big time, I tried for any opening that came along – *Practical Caravan, Readers' Digest, Knitting & Sewing Machine Times*. The symbolism wasn't lost on me, either. Timid, lacking in pride, I didn't have the guts to chase the pretty girls; I chose the plain ones instead in the belief that they'd be flattered, grateful for the attention.

That Monday, tucked away in a corner, was an inch-square ad for an assistant editor at 'Britain's favourite men's magazine'. What made me look twice was the absence of any outrageous demands for qualifications, graduate status or 80 w.p.m. typing speed.

Not that I'd ever considered porn as a career. That wasn't the plan at all. Novelist fame, that's what I wanted. I'd spent years at it already, hundreds of lonesome hours at the typewriter, fuelled by tea and cigarettes, a one-bar electric fire under the table to toast my toes. A classic scenario. Sometimes, though, the vision wobbled. The vertical hold went haywire. It seemed so hopeless that I had panic attacks, waking in the middle of the night: twenty-nine and I had only pennies to my name. And a £45 overdraft. Every time the bank wrote me a letter I shoved it in the bin. Whenever I had to pass the NatWest I crossed the road, convinced that if the manager saw me from his window, he'd rush out and make a grab for me.

Getting the *Fiesta* job would be ideal. I'd make easy cash bashing out sex rubbish, then hurry home at five to carry on with the serious stuff. The strategy had honourable precedents, cool writers like Henry Miller and Anaïs Nin who'd eased their poverty by penning erotic stories for rich perverts.

For a natural slacker like me there were other attractions. The *Fiesta* offices were only a two-minute bus ride from Belsize Park. No jam-packed Tube trains full of sweat and garlic breath, no being jostled around the West End like an unpopular rugby player. I could get up as late as 8.30, throw down coffee and a slice of toast and still get to work on time.

Girlie-mag titles – *Mayfair*, *Penthouse*, *Playboy*, *Park Lane* – smack of high-life fantasies. It's not fraud, exactly. The readers, eager to believe, are as much to blame, picturing plush offices staffed by suave journos, the fragrances of fresh coffee and Chanel, a constant traffic of snooty models and gorgeous secretaries. And reality? Galaxy Publications was housed in, appropriately enough, an old underwear factory. The ground floor was occupied by a garage and crowded around it were a pub, a greasy-spoon caff and a second-hand furniture shop. Anonymity was the order of the day, hence the unmarked doorway. Between walls glistening with the thick green and chocolate paint of old primary schools, an uncarpeted stairway led up to the first floor. There were no potted palms, no leather sofas, no bunnies with top-class dentistry. There was just Janice.

So here I sit clutching my portfolio: poems from the school magazine, two travel pieces from the *Observer*, and some smutty stories I'd written for another girlie-mag company who'd put an ad in *Time Out*. The door-lock buzzes and a blonde in a sloppy rugby shirt beckons. As I follow her through, the clatter of typewriters stops and I put on my dopey smile, conscious of all eyes on me.

Those who despise the producers of porn might not be so reverent, seeing not smoothies but demons. Ask for a thumbnail sketch of an editor and it would probably include every cliché: an unironed shirt with buttons on threads, tie with dried splatters of egg (which he picks off and nibbles), rubbed-off corduroys with dubious stains, pseudo-snakeskin shoes and psychedelic socks – the whole ensemble imbued with a certain smell, not disgusting exactly, but not pleasant either, an uneasy mixture of soap and sweat.

Not this chap. Tall, angular, bespectacled, in a metal-buttoned blazer, surely he'd be more at home hosting a quiz show on TV. His long fingers look perfect for framing rectangular question cards. Offering me a seat at the side of him, he dispatches his secretary to fetch two coffees.

'Have you worked for a magazine before?'

'Er, no, not really. I had some stuff in the *Cygnet*.'

'*Cygnet*? What's that? Something to do with bird-watching?'

'My old school magazine.'

He stares at me as if I'm mad. For a second I expect to be shown the door, chucked headfirst down the stairs before I've even got the taste of coffee on my tongue. In fact, yes, I'd rather take the physical violence, it wouldn't hurt half as much as that look of disappointment. I so desperately want to be taken seriously, not dismissed as a time-waster.

'It wasn't the sort of thing I was thinking of,' he says drily. 'To be honest, we were looking for someone with a bit more professional experience.'

Shit! Why did I mention the bloody *Cygnet*? I nearly forgot my quality stuff. 'I've had two articles in the *Observer*,' I say hurriedly.

'The *Macclesfield Observer*, is that?' He smiles at his little joke, but it's not a nice smile.

'No, the real *Observer*.'

I hand over the photocopies I've brought with me and relax enough to bask in the kudos. I can tell he's impressed.

'Anything else?'

'I've written some short stories for Gold Star.'

Before the pub job my flatmate Guy and I had topped up our dole by churning out 1500-word 'confessions' for a company who published a stack of pocket-sized magazines with names like *In Depth* and *Sexpert*. I'd never thought of telling anyone about them, still less of showing them. But luckily the mags had been stashed in a cardboard box under the stairs. I dragged them out, smudged off the dots of mould, and scissored out the ones I'd written.

Inspiration came easily. Belsize Park was that kind of

place, the Sodom and Gomorrah of NW3, a leafy homeland shared by au pairs from France and Finland, would-be actresses from the Central School of Speech and Drama in Swiss Cottage, provincial belles from the Civil Service hostel only six doors away from us, lonely exiles from places like Newcastle and Bristol and Dublin.

To save the fag of invention, Guy and I were able to fictionalize our own encounters. How angry these girls would've been if they'd known – proud feminist Marie-Christine turned into Marie-Louise the sex-mad au pair; shy little Gill from Bristol reborn as Susie, the nurse who couldn't say no; lonely Diane revamped as a randy divorcée. This was kiss 'n' tell before the phrase had even been invented. Not for any fat cheques, either. Betrayal on easy payments. All those precious private moments sold off for a meagre £22.50 a go.

Dennis flicks through the stories and nods his approval. Is he going to interrogate me? After all, what proof is there that I'm the real author? There are no by-lines, apart from Randy Tina or Sultry Paula.

'You're not easily shocked, then? That's good. We obviously have to call a cock a cock in this business. Are you keen to learn?'

I nod. It's beginning to look promising. I lean back and sip my coffee with a degree of ease. Dennis leans across to his desk and opens a drawer cryptically flagged 'NO!' on a sticky label. From it he takes out a handful of snaps.

'How would you handle this?'

He thrusts a slippery Polaroid into my hand and – do I imagine it? – lingers half a second more than necessary on the word 'handle'.

A fat woman poses languidly in black panties and peep-hole bra. Two brown nipples poke through. Greying pubic hair runs like a trail of gunpowder up the pock-marked Somme landscape of her belly. My first reaction is 'Yuk!', but I keep shtum. This is obviously some kind of test. I nod stoically.

'Doesn't bother me.'

A heroic lie. I know full well that this suburban balloon – Toni of Stoke-on-Trent – could easily become a regular visitor in my nightmares, a bloated, mutant Cathy tapping at my windowpanes, begging to be serviced. It isn't so much a young man's aversion to all things fatty, but the camera flash has turned her eyes into red dots and her goofy grin has an unsettling touch of the madhouse about it.

Dennis likes my sang-froid. But I can see I've set him a challenge. He's out to super-disgust me. As he rifles in the drawer again, a strange smile plays on his lips. I half expect him to bring out something in a lead-lined box, something so awful it has to be kept locked away in case the public gets wind of it.

'What about this?'

It's the manager of a building society, or a computer boffin maybe, an earnest-looking chap in steamed-up specs. Except that he's wearing a green baby-doll nightie and sucking simperingly on a very knobbly black dildo – Bradford & Bingley samples the Horn of Africa. Does his wife know? Do his kids know? What about his employers? Doubtless he'd put down golf and stamp collecting under leisure pursuits on his CV. His thin willy hangs forlornly below the hem of his nightie: it looks like a frayed rope with a raspberry glued to the end of it.

'Rather gross, eh?'

'I suppose we have to cater for all sorts.'

A silly cliché, but I guess it's the right thing to say. Dennis nods his grudging respect for my unflappable pose. 'You're right there, Nick.'

He's using my name now. I must have crossed some barrier here.

'Leg men, tit men, bum men. And the rest: transvestites, shoe fetishists, stocking freaks. A lot of our readers like historical stuff—'

'Historical?'

'Bloomers, corsets, stockings like the nit nurse used to

wear. All that nostalgia stuff. Every punter's got a thing of his own. Our job is to keep them all hard and happy. What we don't do is make judgements.'

As he talks he slips a Jiffy bag from the drawer, and the next thing I know he's thrust something frilly and slippery into my hand. It's a pair of panties. But there's something else. I recoil instinctively and throw them on the floor. Dennis smiles in triumph.

'Gotcha!'

I feel well and truly sick. The panties are soiled with a dried lump of something brown. Dennis picks them up and takes an appreciative sniff.

'Squashed Mars Bar!' he cackles. 'You're going to have to cope with a lot worse if you come here.'

It's all wrong, topsy-turvy. Dennis shouldn't be here, saying these dirty things to me. He should be fingering the curves of a Victorian butter dish, buffing the brasswork of an ancient flintlock, frightening old ladies with outrageous valuations. What twist of fate has brought him here?

He tosses me a Dunhill and flicks his gold lighter in my face. I light up and manage a weak smile. He takes a deep drag and sits back in his chair to give me the once-over.

Flashback. Grammar school speech day, 1970. I'm walking up on to the stage to collect my prize – best contribution to the *Cygnet*. This is fame's first kiss. From here on in my future's assured: a slim volume of poetry, a column in the *New Statesman*, appearances on *Panorama*.

It never turned out like that, though. Regardless of the flurry of rejection slips, I told the people in the factory where I worked that I was a writer. They smiled in a kindly way and raised eyebrows to each other behind my back. I hated those two-faced smiles. I'd show them.

But fame wasn't the one who kissed me now: I was struggling in the embrace of an old tart who smelt of sherry and face-powder. But I was grateful for the attention.

'I'll let you know,' says Dennis.

*   *   *

Guy kept his fingers crossed for me. We'd both been drifting for a couple of years. I'd been writing and getting nowhere. Since leaving drama school Guy had done rather better, with a couple of panto parts and a one-second non-speaking cameo in *Some Mothers Do 'Ave 'Em*. But it was hardly the career he'd imagined for himself.

Even so, despite the poverty and the rejections, life was fun. We'd both worked behind the bar at the Belsize Tavern and used our position to flirt unashamedly. I never ceased to be amazed at what daft tactics worked. We handed out packets of crisps on the flimsy pretence that it was a special offer for the woman with the best smile. Even the rudeness of staring could be turned to an advantage if you went over and apologized for doing it, pleading weakness.

Guy started his gigolo career working the deck chairs in Hastings, chatting up every French or Swedish girl in a bikini. Somehow the word had spread in Europe that Hastings was the British equivalent of the Riviera, an English hot spot. The tourists' disappointment made them open to any kind of diversion. I wouldn't say that he taught me all I know, but he coached me on a few wrinkles.

'Don't tell them you were a civil servant. It's a complete turn-off. Where's the excitement? Romance, lies, danger, that's what they want. Tell them you're a writer – they'll love it.'

That I'd never been published was irrelevant. I started lying with hesitance. But Belsize Park was the ideal place to practise. How could we go wrong? I soon lost the guilt, felt happy enough to look them in the eye.

After chucking-out time at the pub, the next stop was usually Conrads, a candle-lit basement bistro where couples went for a pre-shag pasta if they weren't in too much of a hurry. (Candle-lit sounds great, but these candles gave off such a stench they must have been made from skunk fat or something.) Since Conrads had an extended licence, most customers just came for more drinks. The basement was full of sozzled loners. Once, someone sloped forward over the table, ignited their hair on a candle, then leaned back in blissful ignorance. Had it been a sitcom the obvious answer would have been to throw a pint of beer over the victim. But I liked my beer too much for that. Instead, I went across and patted the man's head as if he were a patient toddler. His hair crumbled under my fingers. And the smell was hardly conducive to the enjoyment of pasta.

Getting girls into bed was only part of it. I wasn't out to fill a scorecard. Basically, I just wanted these girls to like me, love me, approve of me. I still believed in the sugar and spice theory of girls. I was always on my best behaviour. I never swore, always washed, dreaded a breakaway fart. I tried to treat them like princesses. It made me mad as hell when I saw one of them go off with an unwashed scrounger. Where had I gone wrong?

Sometimes it was a girl's name that made me fall in love – Nancy, Rachel, Susan, Claire. It was a vital part of the attraction, as much a part of the girl's femininity as her hair, her breasts or her voice. I could never have dated a girl with an off-putting name (Sharon, Tracey, Lesley, Marion).

Looking back at my diaries for that period, the pages, in inks of mauve and turquoise and green, are a pot pourri of names and half-remembered afternoons. A pot pourri is not so twee a description: I can still smell those damp autumn afternoons and humid summer evenings, the lingering aromas of spag bol, Earl Grey tea and cigarette smoke; the phone sitting on the hessian carpet like a fat red frog, Guy and me waiting for it to ring.

It was hard to believe the dozens of people who traipsed in and out of our flat. They all had their reasons. Some dropped in for a cuppa or to see what nosh was going free. Some came for a shoulder to cry on. Some came for sex. Some even came to stay.

China, for instance, was just a friend of a girl we met on a late-night Brighton–London train. How such a random encounter led to some third party moving in I can't imagine. But we were chancers. It suited our pose to have girls hanging out of every port-hole. We loved shocking the customers of the Belsize Tavern, turning up every other night with a different girl, spinning myths around ourselves. What sweet revenge to see the looks of envy. So what if we didn't have a decent job or a pension scheme, we looked like we were having fun!

Apart from a carrier bag full of knickers and bras and a UB40, China's only possession was a small electronic keyboard. Pursuing vague ambitions to be a pop star, she spent hours sitting on the floor hunched over it, her face veiled by a curtain of black hair as she plinked and plonked her way through a repertoire of self-penned suicidal bedsitter anthems.

But China wasn't up for any hanky-panky. She had no money to pay for food or rent, but she wasn't going to pay in kind either, so dashing Guy's hopes.

Charlotte, the girl from Swiss Cottage Library, was a touch more communicative. One day, while he was having his books stamped, she told Guy she'd just been kicked out by her boyfriend. Guy invited her to stay and the next day she turned up with a duvet and a multicoloured umbrella. This time Guy was luckier. But a week later her boyfriend came to fetch her back. Her bluff with the jealousy card had been a success, but Rory – how we'd laughed at the poncey name! – was so angry he thought I was the one who needed to have his face bashed in. I managed to save my nose from a complex fracture, but Charlotte was so pretty I would have happily borne such an injury for the chance of bedding her.

We shared a kitchen and bathroom with Babs, a thirtyish actress. She affected classical leanings, but all we'd seen was her downtrodden Mrs X in a telly ad for aspirins. We took phone messages for her, but none was ever from Trevor Nunn.

Neither of us had ever tried it on. We felt sorry for her.

Too squeamish. An unspecified childhood accident had left her with a neck like frazzled Wensleydale, scar tissue hidden from public gaze by the artful employment of chiffon scarves. We speculated how far this scar extended.

Babs had a strangely ambivalent attitude to us, forever barging into the bathroom when one of us was in. Our protests were dismissed with ironic laughter: 'Oh, boys! Don't flatter yourselves. Your nakedness means nothing to me. You know I prefer older men . . .'

But one day she got us drunk on some sickly orange liqueur and persuaded us to strip for a snapshot. Under her direction I sat at the typewriter, while Guy stood behind me, looking on with amiable interest. Now, what that was all about, and where the photographs are, I'm not sure.

A week after the interview Dennis rang and told me I'd got the job – on a fortnight's trial. The *Observer* cuttings together with the porno stories had clinched it. Literate enough not to be a pervert, corrupted enough not to come over all saintly, I was just the kind of guy they wanted.

That evening, leaning at the bar of the Belsize Tavern, drunk on lager and self-confidence, I was, in Billy Liar mode, already a journalist of some repute. I found 10p and rang my mum on the pub payphone. 'Mum, guess what.' I jammed a finger in my ear to block out the rattling thump of the jukebox. 'I've got a job! Assistant editor on a magazine.'

'Oh, I am pleased. Where is it?'

I couldn't tell her it was on a girlie mag! She'd have a fit. What would she tell Auntie Ivy? What would she think of me, my attitude to women? I had to think quick.

'On the *TV Times*.'

I was so cocksure of my own brilliance that I didn't find out till much later what kind of rivals I'd been up against. Hardly anyone serious, it seemed. An ad in the *Sun* for

Prime Minister could hardly attract a more mixed-up bunch of egotists and salvationists.

To be honest, I was probably just the best of a poor bunch. Half my rivals were utter wankers, with not a jot of journalistic skill between them. Simply being a sex maniac was the perfect qualification, or so they thought. Others were sad and suspicious: why would a fifty-four-year-old editor of a yachting magazine want to move over to the twilight world of girlies?

And there were always a few more just like me, desperate to get into the media, hence the pile of exquisitely typed CVs from recent graduates. But what kind of career could this be for a young man who'd spent the last three years studying the Classics? Was he getting *Fiesta* mixed up with something else? Did he imagine our nudes were all as classical and hairless as the Venus de Milo? How could such an aesthete handle a bollock-naked Tracey with boobs like medicine balls?

In any case, as Dennis so succinctly put it, he didn't want any 'smart Alec brainboxes with high-falutin ideas'.

2 Deadlier than the Mail

My first job at *Fiesta* was knocking together the letters pages.
A routine task, but a vital one. Naked women are an obvious
lure, but girlie mags have a literary function too. The filth
and frankness of readers' tales was, still is, a key factor in the
popularity of titles like *Fiesta* and *Knave*. Stitched together,
side by side, a labour of love, they make a Bayeux tapestry
of modern life, animated by mythic figures: the randy housewife, the willing au pair, the horny workman, the sunbathing
neighbour, the laundry-basket sniffer, the knickerless secretary. Half the readers can't stop writing, the other half can't
wait to lap it up. Perfect symbiosis. And superbly cost-
effective: six pages of bone-on editorial copy, absolutely free.

'You make them all up, don't you?' demanded Tone and
Phil at the bar of the Belsize Tavern.

Me and my big mouth. Why did I have to be so vainglori-
ous? Working in porn was one thing, boasting about it was
reckless. From then on a quiet pint would always be out
of the question. Tone scrunched out his fag in the ashtray
and gnawed greedily at his cheese and onion roll, still ex-
haling smoke as he masticated.

'Come on, it's a bloody leg pull.'

I didn't yet know it, but this sceptic routine would be
repeated ten thousand times from then on. Despite my protests Tone and Phil (and all those who echoed them) refused
to believe that anyone, any member of the public, any normal bloke, would actually sit down with paper and a biro
and write such letters.

Tone and Phil had had their noses in girlie mags for years – required reading for tea breaks in the building trade. Naked women were the working man's frieze, pinned, sellotaped and Blu-Tacked to the walls of ten thousand garages and site huts, toasted in pot-sized mugs of stewed PG Tips. That was normal enough and they happily confessed to it.

'Can't blame a bloke for looking, eh? It's bloody nature, innit? Fuck the bloody feminists.'

'No thanks, Phil. Never fuck anyone in a boilersuit, that's my motto!'

But they'd have hated anyone to think they'd stoop to writing dirty letters. Those kind of men, they were sad, frustrated wankers – 'flagpole polishers' Phil called them – so hard up for a thrill that writing FUCK was the dirtiest, daringest thing they could think of. Those kind of men had poofy leather purses with a zip-up section full of 10p coins for heavy-breathing phone calls.

'I reckon some of them blokes need treatment,' said Tone. Phil nodded in agreement. They still only grudgingly believed me. 'Who'd write that kind of stuff?'

Men did it, but Tone and Phil were desperate to shift the guilt. *Fiesta* and *Knave* and people like me were there to take the rap. We wrote the mags, didn't we? We offered women money to get their kit off and took photos of them. We printed the mags, delivered them, put them up on newsagents' shelves. You couldn't blame ordinary blokes like Tone and Phil and their mates for buying them. They loved the whole bargain-priced package – the birds, the letters, the dirty jokes – it was like properly printed 'official' support for their creed, the brickies' *ABC* of ale, baccy and cunt. But they couldn't bring themselves to admit that they (along with another 200,000 *Fiesta* readers) were mixed up in the conspiracy too.

It soon sank in: I'd only gone and got myself a job as a scapegoat, a patsy for a nation of guilt-ridden males. But I really should have known: the prostitute always gets the blame.

'Come in and have a look,' I insisted. Tone and Phil were working on a building site at Swiss Cottage, just down the road. 'Pop down for a lunchtime drink. I'll give you a guided tour.'

I wanted them to see for themselves: my desk was piled high with folders, one for each month's worth of letters, all stashed full to bursting. Sheets of pale blue Basildon Bond, pages torn from ring-binders, flimsy aerograms, left-over Christmas cards, cutie squirrel notelets – anything that came to hand – they could all be used to write in with a message. Even headed notepaper from the House of Commons:

> . . . during PM's Question Time the House was
> blissfully unaware of the secret thrill I got from
> wearing those creamy silk camiknickers
> beneath my Tory pinstripes . . .

So maybe it wasn't the brickies and truck drivers, after all. The handwriting hinted at all social classes, all ages, all levels of literacy. Some of it looked as sweet and neatly looped as a virgin's diary – at first glance. It came as a double shock to find words like fuck and prick and arse hiding in there, scrolled in disciplined copperplate but as alarming as barbed wire. The lady teachers who'd taken such pains with those boys would have died to see it used for such filth. At the other extreme the writing was tight-arsed and buttoned to the throat, block capitals as fiddly as hallmarks on a ring, so tiny you'd need a magnifying glass to decipher them.

Most appropriate was the stuttering black biro style. You could just see it: the ink's running low and the ball's sticking, but the writer's just too excited to notice. Such dreadful symbolism: proud virility let down by faulty pipes and shoddy workmanship.

They weren't all in longhand. More pretentious writers,

in a vain attempt to distance themselves from the scrib-
blings of perverts, aimed for a spurious hint of authority
by using a typewriter:

> . . . I'm dictating this to my secretary so she can
> confess to your readers what a sex-mad tart she
> is underneath her prim white blouse and
> pleated skirt. When she has finished this she
> will attend to her other secretarial duties (if
> you know what I mean!) . . .

But no secretary would own up to this work. One look
was enough to suss the pressure-cooker frenzy. You could
almost hear the valve jiggling crazily on its loosened screw.
All the holes in the 'o's, 'b's and 'p's were bashed out, so
the paper looked like a tea-shop doily. Where do they get
this low-grade stationery from? Hold it up to the light and
it's like a do-it-yourself planetarium show revealing
the weird and unmapped constellations of the human
brain.

Some letters were terse and action-packed – 'She came
round. I pulled off her knickers. I fucked her. She bucked
on the bed like a rodeo horse' – thumb-flip cartoons that
were over in seconds (much like the writer himself, I
guessed). Others were long and slow, covering pages of
quality notepaper, unbuttoning their details as carefully as
a woman's blouse. These men didn't make Neanderthal
attacks, they stood in awe, babbling about 'soft and wonderful breasts', describing each puckered and goosepimpled
nipple in loving detail. They felt genuinely privileged to be
allowed entry to their girlfriends' 'honeyed pleasure gardens'. Unlike the Neanderthal, they didn't look at their
watch afterwards and piss off, they stayed and made a pot
of tea.

One or two pieces of paper breathed perversity: weird
block-capitalled green ink stuff that you knew wasn't right.

Desperate Maydays from lonely rooms, they were imbued with the lingering bedsit aromas of gas and old Heinz tins. Fingerprints too, filigreed in dried out spunk maybe, as dead and murky as tallow. I soon got used to it. Mostly it was Carry On stuff: mad, bad, but hardly dangerous.

So, if it wasn't Tone and Phil, who was it?

A truism: real-life murders never conform to the penny-dreadful cliché. The same goes for the readers of girlie mags. The all-purpose pervert in a greasy mac, brown lace-ups and bottle-thick specs is just a decoy, a figure of urban mythology. A convenient one, too. As long as we have this fictional fall-guy, the real culprits dodge the spotlight. Not that anyone's ever confessed to me, but I know that these letter writers could be anyone: the old gent next door, the well-mannered lad at the bus stop, the milkman, the bank cashier, the lollipop man. They've always been out there. They're out there right now. All across the country, men slip off the familiar masks of dads and grandads, husbands and boyfriends, and slope off to the garden shed or up to their dens to suck their pens (whoa! careful there, type-setter!) and commit their fantasies to paper. Yes, I'm talking about you, S.B. of Dorset:

At 72 I thought I was past it, but after seeing
your six-page spread about Directoire knickers
I've just given the wife the best seeing-to since
VE Day!

And you, Ken of Leeds. And you, Mick the Masturbator of Tunbridge Wells. It's a wonder you've got enough saliva left to lick the stamp.

I thought Tone and Phil would jump at the chance of a visit to the office, but they came over all shy at my sugges-tion. Just as well, I concluded. Quite what Dennis would have said when two men with sweaty T-shirts and mud-caked boots turned up, I didn't dare imagine. He wouldn't be rude, not to their faces, but he'd have had a fit on me. It's one thing producing mucky mags and pretending to be matey with the readers, but you didn't need to host open days for them.

Doing the letters seemed, on the face of it, a pretty straightforward task. Hardly journalism, more a clerical routine with a bit of typing. But my first batch was a disaster. Desperate to impress Dennis with my attention to detail, I spent hours on it. Sensibly sequenced paragraphs, proper quote marks, carefully considered semicolons – I'd brought order out of chaos, made filth squeaky clean. Apart from the odd blot of Tipp-Ex it was a work of art.

In Dennis's office I stood by, proud but nervous, while he gave my work the once-over. He started off making little ticks with his green biro, then he sighed heavily. I couldn't see his eyes face-on, but I caught the glint of anger reflected in his specs. My heart sank. The green pen started slashing through whole paragraphs.

'Incest – no. Buggery – can't have that. Schoolgirls – Jesus Christ!'

He grabbed another Dunhill from his packet and snapped the flame to it. Training raw recruits obviously had a bad effect on his nerves.

'We can't afford to waste time like this,' he snapped.

I felt sick. I'd seen him glaring at me as I typed. I'd claimed at the interview to be a competent typist, but it was an obvious lie. Now this. I'd been rumbled. I was a timewaster, nothing more than a dreamy kid who'd half-written a bad novel and was arrogant enough to think that journalism was just an easy way to make money. Not real writing. At this rate I'd be out on my ear by the end of the week.

Dennis kept half of the letters and handed the rejects back to me. 'You'd better memorize this,' he said, adding an eight-page set of guidelines to the pile.

Rape, buggery, incest, schoolgirls, oral sex – the law allows us, post *Lady Chatterley*, to write about virtually anything. It's all been done and it's in a novel in your local bookshop, probably by the winner of the Booker Prize and so well crafted you can almost hear the mucous membranes slapping. Write about those same subjects in a girlie mag, though, and you could be in trouble. For W. H. Smith and Menzies the watchword was context – who was doing the writing, in what way, and what an average reader might make of it. Novelists could describe fathers bedding their daughters, but *Fiesta*'s punters couldn't. *Lolita* was acclaimed fiction, but Ron of Basildon's schoolgirl fantasies were the product of a sick mind. One writer enjoyed artistic immunity, the other was condemned as a pervert.

Book readers could be trusted, it seemed, but the men who bought girlie mags were dodgy characters, ready to go off stalking and raping in response to the slightest stimuli. No one ought to be writing about these activities to entertain or, worse, turn people on. But who was to say that the people who wrote and read the novels didn't get a perverse thrill from them? Did literary finesse and good spelling somehow make it all OK? The double standards appalled me.

Galaxy submitted proofs of *Fiesta* and *Knave* to top solicitor Michael Rubinstein for legal clearance, but that was almost a formality. W. H. Smith and Menzies were the ones who made a fuss.

Three proof copies of each issue had to be submitted to a panel for approval. As well as the taboos on the list Dennis gave me, these moral guardians pored over every photograph, alert for vaginas that looked too moist, penises that might be considered (by the jealous or inadequate) as semi-erect. No body contact of any kind was allowed. Recently, one picture with a white blotch on the model's leg had been ordered to be replaced: it could have been misconstrued as 'male semen'. Even four-letter words could get us into trouble if they were used too often or printed in too large a type size (10pt maximum, no usage in headlines or titles).

Protests were useless. In addition to their own shops, Menzies and W. H. Smith also controlled wholesale deliveries to thousands of smaller newsagents. In the old days (pre-1984) this routine often involved frantic taxi rides to the printer's with a replacement picture. Nowadays computers perform miraculous retouching jobs, drying up the glint of moisture, gently reclosing pouting labia, lopping an inch from the middle of a penis and seamlessly joining the two halves again, even changing eyes from brown to blue if it goes better with the decor.

Tears were already welling in my eyes as I walked out of Dennis's office. I was half-ready to hand in my notice. But he hadn't finished.

'And lay off the semicolons. The semicolon has no place in a girlie magazine.' The readers would be too excited to employ such punctuation.

Why the hell hadn't he given me the guidelines before I'd started on my typing marathon? It was as if he was setting me tests, but not giving me any warning.

But now I knew the rules I'd make sure there were no more schoolgirls or landlords who demanded sex in lieu of rent. Since I was genuinely curious there were still questions I wanted to ask – like did incest include men and their daughters-in-law?; was an eighteen-year-old sixth-former still classed as a schoolgirl? – but I now felt too inhibited, too fearful of incurring Dennis's wrath. And it was with some reluctance that I conformed with the moratorium on semicolons.

Until a few weeks previously Dennis had been *Fiesta*'s assistant editor. Now he'd been promoted it seemed he wanted to distance himself from the nitty-gritty. I couldn't entirely blame him. Tapping out readers' letters certainly didn't seem right for an avuncular cove in a metal-buttoned jacket.

Luckily I found myself a mentor. While Dennis tutted at my lack of experience, Colin, my opposite number on *Knave*, was more inclined to help me out. He'd previously worked for Gold Star, the company Guy and I had done our £22.50 stories for, so he already knew my name. I actually had some kind of minor fame as a writer of porn! Moustachioed and laid-back, Colin was a guy I could get along with.

I thought I'd got off on the wrong foot by sniggering at his leather jacket. Some leathers are shamelessly macho, winking with studs, scuffed by countless scrapes along the tarmac. This wasn't one of those: it was a left-winger's leather jacket, effete and as tough as custard skin. It wouldn't survive a tumble off a swing, let alone a spill at the Isle of Man TT. But Colin took my joshing in good humour. Anyway, however soft, his leather was marginally more street cred than my anorak, even if the latter did sport natty blue and red piping from shoulder to cuff.

Colin wasn't that keen on me adopting him as a mentor; he had enough responsibilities. But we forged a survivalist friendship based on a love of books and films. Wobblingly fortified by piles of books, Colin's corner was a homage to film noir. Alongside stills from stylish gangster movies and Hitchcock thrillers, women like Bette Davis and Ingrid Bergman stared down at us, erotically veiled in smoke from Colin's Gauloises.

Colin had a great line in caustic wit, much of it aimed at the *Knave* editor, who was scarcely ever in. After choosing the month's pin-ups he'd leave a pair of glasses on his desk to give the impression he'd just popped out for ciggies. No one could say anything because he was a friend of the boss's from way back. But Colin was well able to cope. He'd been in the business long enough to do it on auto-pilot.

Belsize Park was full of foreign girls working as au pairs, students, exchange teachers, auxiliaries and cleaners. You could spot them a mile off: every evening they formed a chattering queue outside the local call-box, phoning home to complain about homesickness and nasty employers. They were all clean and bright, but forced by various laws to stay on the bottom rung of the employment ladder.

Marie-Christine, for instance, French and blonde and the first girl I'd ever met who admired Jean-Paul Sartre.

We clicked when she turned up one day to clean our kitchen. As some kind of legal dodge our landlord provided 'bed and breakfast' – a Kellogg's Variety pack, a thimble of milk, and a cube of butter which got put at the bottom of the fridge and eventually turned into a rancid turd. The dodge meant he also had to provide fresh bed linen and someone to hoover up. Recent recruits had included a gay Indian and a Spanish girl with a hairy mole. Marie-Christine was the first normal-looking person we'd had and I was chuffed when she agreed to go out with me.

Poor girl, she was quite baffled when I took her home to the Midlands. Why was everyone so keen to buy her a drink? Being French was enough for the hayseeds in my local. So what if she wasn't a pin-up, all the more reason to believe it was her magical Continental powers that held me in thrall. French kissing, a bit of French, her folks had taught the dowdy British all the sexual acts they felt so guilty about.

Swedish massage, Turkish Delight, Red Hot Dutch, Danish nurses . . . preface anything sexual with a Continental adjective and, in the eyes of the British, you've got instant sin. Even '69' is reinvented as *soixante-neuf* so we can wriggle out of the blame. And, according to the *Oxford English Dictionary*, buggery is derived from Bulgar. Anyone would think sex had been invented in Europe and smuggled past customs to corrupt our clean-living citizens. We suspect our neighbours of all kinds of kinky stuff; the most innocent aspects of their culture are open to rumour and gossip. Tone and Phil were knocked backwards when I told them I'd been in a sauna in Finland.

'Now, what kind of funny set-up do you call that? Mums and dads, teenage lasses, horny lads . . . be honest, it's got to lead to some kind of shenanigans, ain't it?'

Even the word Continental is *risqué*. At the now-closed Continental Cinema in Tottenham Court Road, where I went for a bit of culture when I first moved to London, I was always aware of impatient shuffling in the darkness. These men were hooked by the Continental tag and paid good money in the hope of a bit of smut. Eventually they stomped out, livid after sitting through two and a half hours of subtitled French and not a single nipple to show for it!

At *Fiesta* and *Knave* we traded on this mythology as much as anyone, adapting it, reinventing it and perpetuating it. It was an easy cop-out. So much easier for us to pretend that the naked blonde was Helga from Oslo and make up a pile of bullshit about her healthy appetite for sex. Finnish girls loved doing it in the snow, German girls loved to bite on glistening bratwursts.

Swedes and Danes and Germans were easy to invent. Some readers preferred their women more exotic. While a few asked for Afro-Caribbean models, they weren't that popular. Whether this was due to racism it's hard to say. And we had no idea what proportion of our readers were black. Oriental girls were more popular, due perhaps to the myth about them being schooled in the art of man-pleasing. Such beliefs must have been anathema to millions of sophisticated women in Kuala Lumpur and Hong Kong, and were unwittingly supported by the hundreds of poor Filipinos who put themselves on the international marriage market.

Few of the foreign girls I knew ever conformed to these stereotypes. The blonde with the blue eyes and impossibly pointed boobs usually turned out to be from Madrid, while the frumpy brunette was – surprise! – the legendary Swedish au pair, fantasy employee of a million husbands, enduring butt of all those dirty jokes.

Having a foreign girlfriend neatly sidestepped the pitfalls of class. When chatting up posh girls who worked for the BBC or the *Telegraph*, though I considered myself their intellectual equal, I always felt lumbered by my Midlands accent. My lines were OK (I'd rehearsed them often enough) but delivered in that deadpan North Staffs way, they didn't exert the magnetism I hoped for. To foreigners, though, accents are much of a muchness. Marie-Christine, far from being snooty, was enchanted: I only had to mutter something like 'I'll go to the foot of our stairs and have a chip butty' and she was putty in my hands.

And it worked both ways. Listening to her accent almost counted as foreplay. Even when she lost her temper and reverted to French, some rough equivalent of 'Nick, you're so fucking lazy and I hate your guts', I couldn't help but experience a *frisson* of sexual pleasure.

But into each romance a little perversion must always creep.

Marie-Christine came from a family of wealthy French truckers (were I still at *Fiesta* I would make a brilliant spoonerism from that, but I must avoid recidivism). Having become a socialist, she felt that a show of penance was called for – hence her job scrubbing floors. A penchant for making love doggy-style was, I'm sure, part of this; an Anglo-French Lady Chatterley thing. At the same time, this humility was hard to square with her feminist principles. Being treated like an impudent maidservant was OK as a guilt trip, but as feminism it looked like sheer hypocrisy.

> Marina sucked him readily, licking and kissing
> along the swollen shaft. Then Jack tensed and
> began to come, gripping Marina's blonde locks
> as she gulped as fast as she could, swallowing
> every drop of his hot seed.

The scenario is an enduring one, a perennial male fantasy. Yet, were it not for the subject matter, the style might almost be Mills & Boon.

Until I met Marie-Christine I'd never had oral sex. I thought it was just a rumour. A willing convert, that first time the orgasmic rush was upon me before I knew it. Still, I was so washed out with the thrill of it, I actually said, '*Merci beaucoup.*' I meant it sincerely, but it sounded awfully flippant.

Marie-Christine gave me a look, but said nothing. Turning her back on me, she began to dress, using the wardrobe door as a screen. I knew I'd upset her. It wasn't as if I'd forced her, or that it had even been my idea, but I still felt bad. I just didn't know the rules. I sat on the bed, dejected and confused. No wonder she hated me. Every guy dreamed of having a girl suck him off, but it was more of a rite than a right.

Then she came and sat beside me, put her arm around me. The angry glint in her eyes had gone. She wanted to kiss – and I was eager to make up. Hell! The kiss was only so she could blow a gobful of spittled spunk back into my mouth. After five minutes of enforced silence she gasped with relief, her face cracking into a malicious grin.

'So, *mon petit roi anglais*, it is a very good vintage, *n'est pas?*'

Groaning at the taste, I ran and spat it all out in the sink. 'Bloody hell, Marie-Christine!' I had to admit though, it was a smashing joke.

Guy and I bedded these foreign girls with casual arrogance. It seemed cynical, but it was of mutual benefit. They used us as much as we used them. What better way to pick up colloquial English and get escorted round London than acquire a native boyfriend. Fucking with the English was a better way to learn the language than attending some sleazy rip-off language school.

But the pleasures they taught us were nothing to do with sex. A French fanny was no different to an English one, Swedish tits no more stunning than British boobs. Mostly it was food they educated us about. Marie-Christine taught me how to emulsify wine vinegar and Dijon mustard; Boel showed us how to get every last shred of meat from a crab's claw and wash it down with ice-cold lager; Evelyn got us smashed on *Kirschwasser*; Pitusa proudly served up real paella (and nearly threw it over us unless we pronounced it properly); and Alice from Delft weighed in with an award-winning tin-opener (made in Holland). We got badges too from Guy's German girlfriend: *'Atomkraft? Nein Danke!'* I wore mine with pride, a double ID, anti-nuclear and bilingual. These girls, through an accumulation of small ways, made us cosmopolitan and European and changed our lives for ever. The sex was a bonus.

Galaxy's premises were, in most respects, indistinguishable from the great archipelago of offices strung across the nation. We were just another business, next door to Decca Records, above a garage, listed in *Yellow Pages* under Publishers. The offices were filled with the smells of coffee and sellotape, the clatter of typewriters, the wall calendars marked with coloured sticky tape for everyone's holidays and dental appointments. Anyone peeping in through a window could easily have taken it for the offices of an importer of bathroom accessories or the accounts section of a building company. There weren't even any pin-ups. The calendars were deadly dull, standard stuff issued by a typesetting company in Finsbury Park, enlivened (if that's the right word) by photos of English stately homes.

Only by visiting the editorial section would you get any inkling of what was going on, by peeping as the lemon-coloured sheets of A4 paper edged their way up out of the typewriters.

The editorial desks formed an enclave of wackiness and mutiny. Since I'd taken his desk Dennis had moved into his own office, a ridiculous glass-walled affair three times as long as it was wide. From there he could assuage his paranoia by keeping an eye on events. Colin objected strongly to this Big Brother surveillance and sellotaped various movie posters to our side of the glass. Dennis could scarcely come on all dictatorial by ordering their removal, but we noticed that one or two had got torn in the corners. We could see the glint of his specs through the paper. Unnerved, I suggested remedial action, but Colin vetoed it. He refused to turn it into some kind of childish feud.

'If he wants to eat paranoia pie let him choke on it. I'll stick to lettuce.'

I didn't see the logic, but I was getting used to Colin's non sequiturs. Whenever I asked dumb questions, like did he prefer blondes to redheads?, he just replied that it was like trying to compare a rusty moped to a commemorative stamp from Monaco. I even kidded myself I knew what he meant.

Most importantly, Colin taught me how much I could get away with. Like lunch-hours, for instance. Dennis was forever fearful of being away from his desk for too long and he expected the rest of his staff to feel the same. Colin warned me not to get drawn into that trap. Keep your head down and don't get involved in office politics was his advice.

Knave was more up-market than *Fiesta*. In the titillation trade every mag has its particular niche. There is a definite top ten, but it's based on hazy values more than sales. *Playboy* and *Penthouse* and to a lesser extent *Mayfair* were, certainly in the eighties, a kind of international royalty. Then came *Men Only* and *Knave*, followed by *Fiesta* and *Escort*. In fact, the sales were in more or less inverse proportion to their poshness. We paid lip service to the beauties in *Playboy*, but we were bored with the rest of it, the high-life tips and interviews with statesmen and writers. The British clung to homegrown stuff: dirty letters, puerile jokes, girls who were randy rather than beautiful.

Fiesta wasn't all tits and fannies, though. Like *Knave*, it had pretensions to seriousness. 'Moving Pictures' was a semi-serious review of cinema. No director was too highbrow – Pasolini, Kurosawa, Fellini, Borowczyk – so long as they had a penchant for nude scenes. The text was written by a respected film buff, but true to his brief, he concentrated his copy on the juicy bits.

Our sources for a typical collage of horny stills were quite respectable – The Kobal Collection, The Cinema Bookshop

– but the quest was unambivalent: anything with tits in, please. We couldn't put it into words – these organizations would have screeched at any hint of collusion with the porno industry – but as long as it remained tacit it was OK: we paid them handsomely, so they swallowed their principles. Anyway, how come they had so many tits 'n' bum stills to lend us?

Fiesta started life in 1968, a by-product of the decade's free-love ethic. The 'i' in the title had been stylized to look like the kind of knob-end you'd see sketched on the back of lavatory doors. Russell Gay had been a photographer, but it didn't take him long to suss out that the real bread was in magazines. He was the first millionaire I'd ever met. But he had no mystique. Portly, with amber-tinted specs, he could have been the manager of a seventies rock band. He rarely interfered with the running of the magazines. In fact, he rarely spoke to anyone at all.

It wasn't that he was aloof, merely shy. One day he came into the loo when I was having a wee, but immediately backed out. If anyone had real need of an executive loo, Russell had. I couldn't blame him: I'd have backed out if I'd seen him at the urinal. What the hell do you talk about, minion to millionaire, as you stand watching the yellow froth eddy round the porcelain?

Yet he wasn't too shy to host high-society orgies, if the rumours were to be believed.

He drove a metallic green Mercedes and lived in a grandiose apartment in Regent's Park. The wallpaper was suede, the housemaids did their work topless, the kitchen had a cocaine-dispensing machine, guests who stayed had their sex recorded by hidden video cameras – there was never any shortage of tall tales.

According to office gossips, his wife was a real swinger, a sexual athlete of unflaggable energy. She'd sucked off a visiting cabinet minister, inserted rubbery objects into the arses of various diplomats, and had strapped on a plastic penis and fucked a well-known lady from TV. I half believed it all, but when she turned up one afternoon to collect her husband she looked more like someone whose favourite pastimes would be knitting and making jam for the WI Easter Fayre.

Apart from *Fiesta* and *Knave*, Russell also published *Video World*. Video recorders were still in their infancy (our landlord was the only person I knew who owned one and video cassettes cost about £40 each) but Russell could see the future: prices would tumble and the demand would soar. The demand for sexual thrills would also soar. Although there was no hardcore on general sale, punters could now get hold of their own copies of *The Devils, Last Tango in Paris* or *Women in Love* to watch in the privacy of their own home. When their favourite naughty bits appeared they could press Freeze Frame and 'enjoy the pleasures of home video in full' – i.e., have a wank.

In the two years I worked on *Fiesta* I don't think I ever exchanged more than half a dozen words with Russell. And that was that first Christmas when he came round handing out the seasonal bonus: Marks and Spencer gift tokens in a manila envelope. Allocated on the basis of £10 per year of service, that's all I got – ten pounds. He shook my hand for a nanosecond, but he had to look at the envelope to get my name right. Still, I had enough for a bottle of wine, a tin of St Michael curry (on which I had a temporary craze) and a three-pack of sensible underpants.

'Are they really real?'

Tone and Phil weren't letting up that easily. But what exactly did they mean? The letters were real enough, in all their multicoloured crinkliness. But what about the tales they told? How could I possibly know? Men were capable of all kinds of wild and wacky fantasies. From the time they competed to be the first to lose their cherry, they'd built an edifice of lies. Their sexual CVs were shakily fictional.

But not always. My own recent experiences in Belsize Park had forced me to believe in characters and behaviour I'd never have credited five years previously.

Married women did seduce teenage paperboys, house-wives did open their doors to the milkman wearing nothing but a nightie. Girls went to work as nannies and ended up being seduced by frustrated husbands, fucked in the shower while the wife was out shopping. Girls even went down on all fours and asked to be treated like an impudent maid being taught a lesson. I'd come across all these things myself, so I was prepared to believe in tall tales.

Whenever I tried to defend the letters by telling them about my experiences, Tone and Phil always assumed I was talking about London. No, some of these things had happened in small British towns, thinly veiled behind the curtains of ordinary-looking houses.

I told them about the night I spent in the nurses' home in Northampton. It made a great story. Getting out unseen next morning had overtones of a Carry On film. But slipping past a room where half a dozen nurses were getting changed I was spotted. PERVERT CAUGHT SPYING ON NURSES – it could have been a police matter if my girlfriend hadn't rescued me. She swore her colleagues to secrecy. Their embarrassment was quickly forgotten in the fun of it all. Everyone did, indeed, love a lover.

These tales made me feel good in the company of guys. A skinny, pasty and unphysical kind of man, who couldn't even grow a moustache till he was twenty-three, I was nervous in the company of men. I didn't crave their approval, didn't want to be like them, but these escapades put me on an equal footing with the gritty types, even made me a kind of hero.

Harmless as they were, Tone and Phil had no imagina-tion. The lack of it crippled them when it came to getting a woman. They'd been fooled into thinking that women were after some kind of hard-body masculinity, but as Guy and I knew, what they wanted most was a laugh and a bit of romance. Even if three-quarters of the letters were fantasy, that meant hundreds of them were true. So where did that leave Tone and Phil? The letters were a constant challenge. No wonder they wanted to believe we made them up. What if it were true that most men had eight inches of proudness? If that was the national average, where did that leave them?

In its way, all this letter-writing is vital work. It's us, the little nation of diarists. Half of this minute-keeping is to do with sex. There's an urge not just to do it but to write about it afterwards, like a post-coital action replay. Why else sell diaries with locks on? Boswell, Pepys, Frank Harris, Alan Clark – lionized literati all; but they all had the same basic urge to record their sex lives as Ken of Leeds, S.B. of Dorset and Mick the Masturbator.

How many wives and girlfriends have had their grunts and wriggles faithfully transcribed for the amusement of the nation? This army of anonymous scribblers seems to be engaged in some mammoth census, chronicling the fantasies and sexual mores of the nation (the male half of it at any rate), detailing not only what they do with their own woman, but what they'd like to do to the one next door and the cashier at the local supermarket.

Despite a belated introduction to oral sex, I'd always considered myself pretty worldly. *Fiesta*'s letters soon shattered that delusion. Simple anatomical preferences like big breasts or long legs were easy to understand, likewise a yen for women in stockings and suspenders. But here were all kinds of peccadilloes.

Even basic one-on-one sex shaded off into all kinds of variations. Screwing the wife of a workmate, a neighbour or even an employer was a common fantasy, wishful thinking fleshed out with a thin but viable story:

I've been working as a part-time gardener for a
well-off couple called Kevin and Paula. One
morning Paula invited me in for a coffee, wear-

ing only a négligé and making no effort to
cover herself . . .

Run-of-the-mill stuff. But there were numerous letters
from men whose top fantasy was to watch their womenfolk
being fucked by another man. Some came across it by accident and stayed bent by the keyhole, worked up into a
sexual frenzy:

Something woke me and I went downstairs to
find my wife stark naked on the carpet, her bra
and knickers tossed on the back of a chair. Jim
had his shirt on, but not his pants and was
shagging the arse off her. I kept dead quiet and
watched, feeling so turned on I started wanking. When Jim had a rest and went to the bog,
I started to go back upstairs. But Louise had
seen me. She informed me that since Jim was
such a brilliant lover he would be taking over
my husbandly duties whenever he was in
town.

Other writers claimed to have instigated proceedings
themselves, enlisting the services of a more-than-willing
mate:

I told Kevin he could visit our house whenever
he pleased. My wife is more than happy with
the arrangement and I love to watch this young
man give my wife the sex she needs.

I'd heard about exotic cultures where men offered their
wives to passing guests; we laugh nervously at such prac-
tices, yet maybe some similar instinct remains embedded
in Western culture too.
If our senior correspondents were to be believed, such

things weren't even new, rather some symptom of eighties decadence. They had similar stories dating back to the pre-war era, the only difference being the way such infidelities were made into costume drama, with fond descriptions of the silk stockings and bloomers, a nostalgia that still made the writers horny half a century later:

> Your younger readers don't know what they're
> missing. The silkiness of a woman's bloomers
> is enough to make me come . . .

From such memories fetishes are easily born.

Feet and shoes were a big turn-on for a significant number of men. We often received rambling five-thousand-word letters full of dainty-footed ladies having their arches and insoles washed and kissed, their toes nibbled and sucked by adoring men. Some even went to naturist resorts and, blind to all the obvious attractions of nudity, sat for hours at a café table watching an endless parade of female feet. Eventually, overcome by desire, they'd have to hurry back to their chalet for a wank. The Chinese had a thing about feet, but if Western culture has tended to overlook the charms of the foot, there was always someone willing to give us a ticking off:

> All you chaps think about is boobs and fannies.
> Fiona, last month, beautiful Scottish lass – and
> you completely ruin my enjoyment by chop-
> ping off her feet! When will you realize that all
> your readers haven't got one-track minds. If
> you continue to ignore the delectable feet and
> toes of your models I will cancel my sub-
> scription!

Even those who would never have considered themselves hard-core foot fetishists paid lip-service to the iconic status of the woman in the stiletto shoes. It seemed that while men easily understood their attraction to boobs and fannies (they at least knew what nature expected of them in that department) they were sometimes troubled by more eccentric desires.

Bondage, buggery and sado-masochism were also taboo in the mags, as were any references to nuns, vicars and schoolgirls. This latter was the most touchy. Letters are one thing, but it's hard to guess how far some men might be prepared to go in reality. Aged twenty I had a heavy-petting relationship with a streetwise girl of fifteen. She was prepared to go all the way, but I chickened out, scared of the consequences. Our parents and our friends, though, saw nothing odd in a man of twenty going out with a fourth-former. Eyebrows would certainly have been raised if I'd been thirty or forty! The raincoated pervert who watches our daughters playing netball is a bogeyman – and rightly so – yet elsewhere this fantasy is slyly kept alive. Amongst the embarrassing visitations offered by strip-o-gram companies, the schoolgirl is always on the menu. No matter that she's no more believable than the kinky policewoman or the randy nurse, she's an enduring icon in the pantheon of sexual stereotypes.

Although 'golden showers' – people pissing on each other – were on the W. H. Smith list of taboo subjects – bursting bladders were OK. The basic story usually revolved around a woman with a bursting bladder, which for some reason or another she was unable to relieve. The accompanying boyfriend, our correspondent, would watch the escaping spots with bated breath. Then, after spinning out the agonizing shopping trip or bus journey for half a dozen pages, relief would come with an earth-shattering orgasmic shower.

Our reactions to the letters ranged from sadness to sickness, but any misgivings I may have had were outweighed by the priceless entertainment. The permutations of human sexuality were a source of endless, often open-mouthed fascination. If I'd landed one of those jobs on *Caravan*

Monthly or *Aluminium World* I'd have been bored to tears after a month.

What a yawning gap there was between most people's love lives and the punter's story, an official report in a barbarian language. CUNT. I hated that word. Even as a teenage L-plate swearer who willingly echoed fuck and shag and fanny, I always shied away from cunt. Those who'd done Chaucer for A level were always eager to remind you of our Anglo-Saxon heritage. Four-letter words were cool. Youth was merely making a post-modernist stand. In medieval London there'd been a street called Gropecuntlane; but by the fifteenth century the word was already deemed obscene and banned from appearing in print. I couldn't say I blamed the authorities. Ugly in sound, full of hatred (had I ever heard it said otherwise?) it gave me an unpleasant *frisson*. Now I faced it every day, cunt in its hundred and one guises: hairy cunt, juicy cunt, pinkly glistening cunt. Cunt. I just couldn't connect it to all those giggling girls in Belsize Park, fresh as daisies in their white blouses and Mum Rolette. I muttered the word to myself, stared at it on the page in the hope I could detoxify it, deflect its black magic, turn it back into a bland arrangement of letters. But the power of that one little word was far too strong.

Worst of all, I couldn't tell anyone the way I felt about it. It'd be the final straw for Dennis: I'd been there a few weeks, but I still felt he didn't trust me. What made me think I was cut out for *Fiesta* if I couldn't stand a simple four-letter word? Even Colin would think me hopelessly prissy.

Prick, by comparison, was full of humour. The heroic acts men attributed to their genitals were full of hilarious vainglory, rarely intentional. These men wanted to put their erect pricks in a trophy cabinet. Indeed, some of them felt compelled to send in proof. Not only would a letter be full of devil-may-care sexual heroism, but we often had a snapshot of the hero – taken via a mirror with a distinctly unsexy background of slacks draped over a chair back. But this 'hero' often bore little resemblance to the prick we'd just read about. Even modern film wasn't good enough to capture the aura of sexual magnetism. These pricks were camera shy. Passed around the girls in the art room, the centre of attention was never the prick – it would receive barely a glance – but everything else.

'My God . . . just look at that awful lampshade.'

Disgust may have been the reaction of some to these letters. But *Fiesta* was, after all, a magazine – why shouldn't its readers write in? If men could dash off a letter to *The Times* to report their first cuckoo sighting, why shouldn't others write to *Fiesta* about their first fuck? The papers were full of opinions on Labour versus Conservative, surely we could tolerate debate on stockings versus tights? Sex was a topic of interest and people had a democratic right to discuss it; if the language was blue and the phraseology reckless, well, that was largely unavoidable.

Prick, fanny, fuck, tits. Men love talking dirty. Simple, single-syllabled, Anglo-Saxon, the words are chanted like a mantra. For some, words are as powerful as pictures. Words cause erections. Cock, spunk, pussy, arse; everyone has their favourites. The seeds are sown a long way back in infancy. Even the mild ones – belly, buttocks, bottom – are just as potent for some men. It's not all anatomy. Brassière, knickers, blouse, skirt – even words like these are lovingly muttered as they are written. Even buttons is a loaded word, full of guilt and half-hidden memories for some.

Our correspondents had created a crazy *mélange* of styles, euphemisms, slang and amateur medical terms. They ranged from the strange poetry typified by such phrases as 'golden globes', 'honeyed love garden' and 'proud nipples', to schoolboy crudities like 'wobbling tits', 'quivering arse' and 'hot juicy twat'. I often wondered who had been the first to use such and such a simile, but girlie-mag lingo had been parroted and recycled so many times that it didn't really matter.

Though frequently cheesed off with the unthinking repetition, I felt obliged to defend the right of these men to free speech. Condemnation seemed to centre on what was, at heart, a basic U and non-U snobbery. A penis was OK, but as soon as a man mentioned his prick, people made automatic judgements about his decency. Making love sounded great – the bookshops were full of manuals which used the phrase incessantly – but it sounded prissy and self-righteous. There'll never be a book called *How to Enjoy a Better Fuck*. But why not? We choose words to define our supposed refinement, but are the couple who make love any happier and well-balanced than the couple who simply fuck? Does 'making love' automatically mean they are in love, as opposed to casual partners who merely copulate because of animal instinct?

Anglo-Saxon sexuality has always been compromised by its vocabulary. Either building-site crude or in pseudo-serious jargon, many of the writers simply did a rewrite along the lines of the last letter they'd read, maybe slotting in the name of the girl in their office in the appropriate places. The same clichés and phrases were recycled in perpetuity. Breasts were always tits or melons; cocks were always eight inches long (the writer's, anyway) and rock-hard; vaginas were always wet and willing.

What was boring for me represented a safe, predictable environment for many of the readers. Every story I sneered at was, for some, an exciting glimpse into a forbidden world of sex which they otherwise had no access to. Like any fantasy world, it had its own time scale, its own laws and code of conduct. Headaches and brewer's droop were unknown. There were no wrinkles or spare tyres, no Caesarean scars, no fatties, no anorexics. The written word beautifies and heroicizes all it describes. Our sexual culture is based on envy. The other man's wife is always sexier, their sex lives always better.

Fashions come and go, even in the world of the perpetu-ally naked. Hairstyles change from beehives to mock-*Dynasty* arrangements; poses and exposures are more or less permissible, depending on the moral climate; even the girls' expressions reflect the zeitgeist: dippy in the sixties, harder in the eighties. But the letters will always be there, no editor would dare meddle with the tradition.

Dennis was a stickler for grammar and spelling. He had a habit of walking up to my desk with galley proofs of readers' letters or 'I Confess' and standing with an impatient expression while I sweated to find what I'd missed. He had me on edge ever since a row in my first week about whether indiarubber was all one word or not and whether it had a capital. Did dildo, like potato, take an 'oes' in the plural? According to the ancient dictionary we had, the plural of vagina was vaginas, but 'Carol and Tina excitedly rubbed their vaginas together' just didn't look right.

I was so eager to please I didn't suss the absurdity of this syntactical obstacle course Dennis made me run. Of course I wanted to be professional, there was no need for sloppiness even in a business like this. I wanted praise for my vigilance. I almost purred when Dennis called me his 'eagle-eyed sub' whenever I spotted something. But at the end of the day, did it really matter? Were readers going to ring in and complain just because I'd missed the hyphen out of One Eyed Trouser Snake?

*   *   *

WE PAY £10 FOR YOUR SAUCY SNAPS!

As if all the letters didn't provide enough entertainment, this reckless invitation brought in a real rag-bag of pictorial stuff. Phallic carrots, bum-shaped potatoes, snapshots of quaint foreign villages burdened with names like Fart and Wank, tourist menus offering delights like 'Shit Kebab' and a 'selection of Danish pansies'. All of these were more or less predictable. But there were some shockers. My own all-time favourite was the Polaroid sent in by a loon who bent himself into a human hoop with the aid of a strong inner tube (round the back of his neck and knees) so he could give himself oral sex:

> As a company director who often finds himself alone in hotels, I recommend this simple kit as the ideal way to relax after a stressful day in conference . . .

Definitely not for publication. As crazy as this auto-fellation was – and I gradually became harder and harder to shock – what puzzled me was the need to take snaps, to record it for posterity. As proof of what? Certainly it would be fascinating to scholars of the future (would they think it was everyday practice in the 1980s?) but what function did it serve now? Hopefully they never got their porn portraits mixed in with their holiday snaps.

Tone and Phil scoffed when I told them about it, so against all professional ethics I smuggled it out of the office and slipped them a look in the pub.

'Fuck me!' said Tone.

They laughed, but were obviously unnerved. The snap was irrefutable proof that perversion existed. It was OK laughing at oddballs who confessed to dressing in their wife's stockings or rummaging through a neighbour's laundry basket, but how many men secretly shared the same desires? D.K. of Luton was easy to mock while he remained anonymous, but what if he turned out to be one of their boozing mates?

Tone and Phil admired my sang-froid. In truth I wasn't any less shocked than they were. Disgusted even. All this was a million miles away from what I expected. Naked women were one thing, a desperate man bound in an inner tube was something else. But what was I going to do?

Resign in protest? For the first time in ages I had money in my wallet and enough 'status' to get a Visa card. Why give all that up for some hazy stance on ethics?

It's not as if Tone and Phil were friends of mine. If they hadn't known me from behind the bar they'd never even have spoken. They'd have classed me as just another Hampstead arty-farty poofter. I didn't mind winding them up with tall tales, but it meant they got too familiar. They thought they could say anything. How could I object? With my CV it was no use making out I was offended.

It wasn't that I thought myself somehow superior to men like Tone and Phil – just more polite. Guy and I sat out on the front steps in Belsize Park and exchanged nods of approval whenever a pretty girl passed by, but we'd never have dreamed of commenting, either as the girl passed or out of earshot. We weren't wolf-whistlers. We'd never say anything like, 'Look at the knockers on that,' or 'Brilliant arse.' We weren't saints, far from it, but we were at ease with our masculinity. Neither of us felt the need to express it loudly as proof.

And more to the point, my agenda was utterly different: I didn't like blondes with big tits. My dream girls wore pink blouses and Laura Ashley dresses; I loved them in jeans and Kickers, I loved them wearing Alice bands and floppy hats. I hated the corrupted fetishistic idea of a woman: leather mini, high-heels, face plastered in make-up, fishnet stockings. Did Tone and Phil really want those fantasy women? Or was it just a show? Conformity is all if you don't want the other guys to suspect you of being a pooftah.

It was bad enough having to stand next to these guys in the urinal. I despised their crude jokes and chauvinistic views; I gritted my teeth and made vague noncommittal noises, but I hated myself for it. This silence was taken as agreement.

Anyway, people like me were the ones who were 'inventing' it all or at least perpetuating it. Sex publishing hadn't grown up entirely unaided: it was a product of peer pressure and dumb acceptance of sexual legends.

Men like Tone and Phil hadn't got a clue – but was it any wonder? They were treated like animals, hustled through life with as much ceremony as sheep going through a dip. Male culture frowned on individuality. Real men never ate quiche, never drank wine, never read novels, never grew pansies, never watched sunsets, never smelt nice. Life was a sequence of negatives, a total denial of enjoyment. They'd been tricked, fucked-up, fooled into thinking masculinity demanded acts of idiocy and hardness. No wonder the Establishment chose men for the army – not so much for their physical strength, but because they followed every order with cheery fatalism.

Real men never kissed either. Kissing was suspiciously close to love, and something rarely ever mentioned in *Fiesta*'s letters and confessions. Foreplay, except as some kind of crude hot-wiring trick, was a waste of time. If you could kick-start women into nymphomania by flicking a clitoris or tweaking a nipple, so much the better. But otherwise the motto was: 'Get in there and fuck 'em.' The only lip contact admitted to was a kind of dental punch-up, a violent tooth-banging tongue-nipping snogging session.

Even going to the toilet was stripped to its basics. You stood in the ranks, staining your soles in the previous piss, watching gobbets and fag ends floating past in the frothing yellow torrent. No wonder men belched and farted to pass the time. No wonder so many wanted to join the army – it must have made them feel at home.

It wasn't just women's bodies that made me gasp, I was endlessly fascinated by their habits and mannerisms, the thousand and one little things that would forever remain a mystery to us men. How did they twist their hair into such neatly symmetrical plaits? Was a slight breeze really enough to make their nipples stiffen? Could they really find men – muscley, hairy, careless with hygiene – as attractive as we found them?

I longed for some of their grace to rub off on me. If I won their approval I knew I must have been OK, a decent chap. To me, male approval was all but useless.

Guy and I, now in our early forties, look back on the Belsize Park days as a golden age. Yet, despite our shared interest in girls, we were both working to very different agendas. Though great friends and flatmates, we were chalk and cheese. I was a diffident, provincial, ex-civil servant; Guy a handsome and confident drama student. On the few occasions we went out as a pair and found female counterparts, Guy usually ended up going off with both of them (and on one occasion even bedding both), leaving me to ponder my shortcomings over a pint.

Abandoned as a toddler, first by his father, then his mother, Guy was brought up mostly by his grandmother. His mother's desertion had the deepest effect. By his own admission, in an article many years later, having so many women and then ditching them was a symbolic revenge. 'What began to emerge was the realization that all my failed relationships with women were part of an inherited destiny,' he wrote.

My mother on the other hand was a heroine who stuck by me. In my adult relationships, I was forever trying to win female approval. Guy looked at a woman and wanted to show her how it felt to be loved; I wanted to show her what a good boy I was. The sex, for both of us, was an essential part of these relationships, but it wasn't the real reason for starting them. Any notches we made weren't for sexual conquests, they were for messages made, approval won.

And these motives were brought into play at every opportunity. Outsiders may have viewed our womanizing as promiscuity – and why disappoint them? But the truth was less gossipworthy: sex was merely a placebo, an illusory remedy to our insecurities.

*   *   *

I'd fancied Elaine for ages, ever since I'd worked in the Belsize Tavern. With her brown wavy hair and Home Counties voice she was ideal: girlish and sexy, and without any of that over-the-top lipstick and fishnets crap.

But whenever she walked into the pub my stomach knotted. The old catch-22: the more I fancied someone, the more I feared rejection. Flirting with foreigners was just a game and no one minded much if it ended up with sex or not. Elaine was different. She looked at me when I looked at her, but I couldn't tell if it was a 'seen enough?' stare or a 'why don't you ask me?' look. Too chicken to risk it, I tried to shrug it off.

Then, one day, I met her in the library and decided to chance it. We went to see *Gandhi* at the Swiss Cottage Odeon and afterwards I suggested a curry.

Guy and myself had another bolt-hole, a local Indian restaurant. Our usual waiter we nicknamed Kew, from his clipped way of saying 'thank you' every five minutes and beaming with anxious servility. We liked him, but his puppy-like eagerness made us uncomfortable. Nor were we so keen on his 'uniform' – red waistcoat and black trousers, shiny with splashes of vindaloo.

What I hated most was the way in which some people lapped up this servile attitude. Most notable were the two famous British film stars who turned up now and then, half-sozzled, knocking over half a dozen dustbins in their clumsy efforts at parking the Rolls-Royce. The plummy-voiced one used the curry house as some kind of revenge trip on uppity Indians.

'Your father was my father's servant,' he reminded the manager. 'And he wasn't so damned slow with the pickles.'

The manager smiled and nodded, but below the bar he wrung his glass cloth into a ligature. I constructed dramatic film scenes in which the manager returned with the man's Barclaycard and, still smiling, whipped the sharp edge across his throat.

If Guy or I was at a table with a girl, the plummy-voiced

actor invariably turned his attentions to us. 'Young men and their love lives,' he grumbled, the night I was in there with Elaine. 'No charm nowadays. No finesse. Let's get a curry and go back for a shag! Look at that one, in here every week with a different piece of totty.'

I tensed with embarrassment. If he spoiled my chances now I'd kill him. Fortunately his ravings were quickly diverted by any shortcomings in the service.

'Call this mango chutney? Tastes like bloody marmalade past its sell-by date. I want hot fruitiness!'

I paid the bill and we left. Neither of us said anything: she just walked with me in the direction of the flat. I hadn't been expecting her to stay the night, not on the first date, but I was happy she did. It all sounds pretty casual, but it wasn't really.

Elaine told me she'd fancied me for ages, hoping I'd ask her out. I could have kicked myself. Shyness was such a curse, a self-inflicted crime of the stupidest kind. I'd wasted days, months of an ideal relationship.

Back in the Midlands I was a bit of a hero.

'Heard about Nick? He works for one of them girlie mags. *Penthouse*, innit?'

They pictured a cocktail lifestyle, pots of money, endless dates with London dolly birds. I felt no urge to put them right while they pressed free pints on me, eager for me to spill the beans. They lapped it all up. Yes, at Galaxy, instead of a canteen, we had a room put aside especially for staff to have it off when they got too worked up by their jobs (the boss even provided free contraception). The boss had Christmas parties, to which all were invited and everyone provided for. The house had all kinds of rooms and you were allowed to wander at will, choosing girls for yourself or watching others at it if you preferred.

Such bullshit all came a little too easy. The free booze quickly went to my head. I found myself saying quite out-rageous things, just to make them laugh. Yet I couldn't shake off the uneasy feeling that I was being their stooge. I thought they envied me, but maybe they despised me too. It wouldn't take much to see through the pretence: if I was so rich and fuckworthy, why was I standing around in a poky pub in the Midlands drinking a pint of warm ale?

3 Next, Please!

Leading glamour magazine urgently seeks models. No experience required.

Luckily there's never been any shortage of women willing to strip off for a few quid. Supply has always exceeded demand. For every one who makes some kind of dodgy on-and-off-benefit living from it, there's always another half dozen who fancy their chances. Each week two or three hopefuls turned up in Galaxy's reception in response to the above advert.

Pin-ups? This lot? Dressed in jeans and trainers, nervously dragging on a No. 6, flicking through the dog-eared mags, they looked like people awaiting the results of a cancer test. Who were they anyway, these girls? Unknown, unconnected, they'd literally walked in off the street. They all had their reasons. Single mums desperate to fund new shoes for the kids. Brassy teenagers who fancied themselves as sex symbols. Reluctant wives bullied by husbands who saw some extra beer money in it.

Perhaps they believed in osmosis, that some of our glamour would rub off, stick to them like glitter, make them sparkle. But we had none to give. Galaxy wasn't that kind of place. All those fantasy high-life furnishings – potted palms, plush carpets, studded leather sofas – were noticeably absent. There was no warm welcome. Not even a warm coffee. These girls wouldn't even get paid.

Janice dished out the standard Model Release Form and watched while they filled it in. She didn't bother to hide her disdain.

'I'll have my pen back if you don't mind.'

No sisterly empathy was apparent. They were letting the side down. A girl's breasts were private, precious, priceless – not a bloody sideshow for a load of perverts and apes in overalls. If they were that hard up why didn't they get a proper job? McDonald's was always on the lookout. Either that or get married. Stripping off was for slags.

Janice dreaded walking past the garage downstairs. Sometimes she walked around the block and approached from the opposite direction, just to avoid it. The wolf whistles she could knock back with a cheerful 'fuck off!'; what offended her was the sellotaped gallery of pin-ups. Not that she was a hard-nosed feminist or anything – she hated 'fat lezzies in boilersuits' as much as strippers – but she couldn't parrot a thesis-length spool of dialectic reasoning to back her views up. She just knew it was wrong. What was the point in her spending all that money on smart blouses, decent skirts, clean tights when all those slobs saw was a fanny on legs?

Now and then one of the novices got cold feet. When Pam, the Geordie 'Model Co-ordinator', came to fetch them they'd mumble some excuse before hurrying out, never to be seen again. Janice's mockery chased them down the stone stairs.

'Who'd want to see her nudity anyway? Spotty-arsed cow.'

For the rest it was too late. When Pam beckoned they meekly followed, down to the studio at the back of the building. The tiny changing room – not much more than a cubby-hole with a curtain – had a dusty mirror and a single chair. The shelf above the dressing table was cluttered with the nuts and bolts of a life in the buff: an encrusted jar of nail polish; a lost ear-ring; yellow-tinted Q-tips no one had bothered to clear away; even the occasional toe-nail, snipped out of the picture at the very last minute. Here the hopefuls stripped off their jeans and T-shirts, avoiding the reflection of their nudity. Until then stripping had been a private act, witnessed only by the mirror or a boyfriend. For some, no doubt, the act was akin to infidelity, a *frisson* of shame and excitement mixed.

Geoff, our studio manager, busied himself setting up cameras and lights. Studio manager sounds grand but, in Geoff's case at least, it was a dogsbody job that called for a variety of skills. From simple dilemmas like deciding whether the girls get Hob-Nobs or Jammy Dodgers with their tea, to practical problems like finding the end on a roll of sellotape. But give him a saw, a paintbrush and a pot of glue and Geoff turned into a wizard, creating amazing illusions from the simplest accessories. A roll of Regency-striped wallpaper and a chaise longue and – hey presto! – we had the boudoir of an eighteenth-century dandy; a pack of Bacofoil and a panel of knobs off a junked hi-fi was easily transformed into a futuristic space-travel set. How reassuring: wherever and whenever the punters roamed in the space-time continuum, there'd always be naked women.

Geoff knew a bit about cameras too. When it came to talking apertures and f-stops and the benefits of Ekta-chrome, he could bore with the champions. More than any-thing, he aspired to be the main man – the laid-back photographer with his team of loyal girls. Dennis didn't trust him that far. But he allowed him limited autonomy for the test-shots. It wasn't much more difficult than taking tourist snaps in Trafalgar Square.

'Ready, then, duck?'

If there'd been an award for the world's slowest strip, these girls would have won it. Naked and nervous (and who wouldn't be in front of critical strangers?) the hapless novice peeped shyly around the curtain – until Pam flung it aside in a rattle of hooks and pushed her into the glare of the spotlights.

It's a funny thing, this commodity called nakedness. Being sexy in the bedroom, stripping off for a lover is easy. But to be naked and at ease in front of a camera calls for a certain talent. Few of these girls had it. Without make-up, with pimples and blotches, tomboy's tits and unruly pubes, they looked stiff, awkward and vulnerable; as erotic as a photo in a medical tome. They had off-putting marks too: a Caesarean scar, bruises from a bully-boy lover, the 'hands off!' brand of a love-bite.

'Give us a smile, then,' Pam would urge.

They tried their best. Some pouted, mimicking pictures they'd seen somewhere. But it just didn't look right.

Left to Pam, these hopeless sessions would have been wrapped up there and then. She knew what Dennis liked. These girls stood no chance. Not even of making a bit of pin-money; their nakedness was completely unsellable. But they had to go through with it for politeness' sake. God owned the original copyright, but now it had been signed over to Galaxy Publications Ltd. The would-be model had sold her sweetest secrets and got nothing in return. The test-shots went into the filing cabinet and stayed there, forgotten. But not before the girls in the office had passed judgement. They who never took off their own clothes got a good laugh out of the desperadoes who did.

'You'd think she'd have trimmed her pubes,' Pam said to Karen, one of the secretaries, as they sat with their coffee and biscuits for a bitch. 'Blokes don't want to see ginger fuzz like that, do they?'

Karen snapped off a finger of Kit-Kat. 'Looks like fucking settee stuffing!'

'She's quite nice,' I protested.

Pam and Karen gave me a pitying look. Blokes! As long as it had boobs and a fanny they'd fuck it. It took other women to make a true appraisal of talent. What made it fun was the lack of guidelines: if a girl was ugly she got laughed at, if she was pretty she got shredded for her snootiness.

A couple of weeks after her audition I saw the girl with the ginger pubes in the Kilburn High Road Argos. She looked up from her catalogue and half-recognized me. After collecting her order – a mains hedgecutter – she walked past and looked again. I knew straight away she'd guessed: I'd seen her naked. And she despised me for it. In that long bustling High Road I was the only man who'd seen her naked. That wasn't why she hated me: it was because she'd got nothing for it. She was woman enough to be looked at by anyone with nothing better to do, but not quite good enough to be paid.

Most men would envy Geoff his job, but he never took advantage. He kept a gentlemanly silence about the sights he'd seen, never gossiped and sniped like Pam and Karen. What his own sexual preferences were nobody really knew. He wasn't gay, but neither had anyone ever seen him with a girlfriend. Perhaps he just enjoyed his job and took his thoughts (and a few spare Polaroids) home with him.

My first objective encounter with nudity was a fat medical textbook I found at my granny's. Its pages contained unsettling hints of mortality: sectionalized livers, disembodied hearts, eyes hanging from bloody nerves. I'd have slammed it shut and never looked again if I hadn't seen the two full-page monochrome plates. The woman had lipstick and a forties hair-do. Her breasts were bare, but between her thighs there was nothing but a clumsy smudge. The man looked a bit like Ivanhoe off the telly, but the publishers were so coy about his manhood they'd drawn a pair of underpants on him. And this in a medical textbook. Despite this lack of detail, I was fascinated. I sneaked a look whenever I went round.

'Can I go in the front room and read *Treasure Island*?'

'Of course you can, lovey.'

See how it happens? For one more hapless kid, guilt and deception had already become part of the experience.

Only in retrospect did I think of the questions. If the publishers could go to the trouble of drawing underpants on the man, surely they could have extended the same courtesy to the lady, given her a nice pair of Marks and Spencer panties? Why was it necessary to erase the vagina altogether, rub it out with the ham-fisted spite of a kid with a rubber? I pondered the anomaly for years before I figured it out. Far from being a sinister plot by a patriarchal society, it was actually based on some kind of twisted chivalry: for technical reasons they could only draw in black – and black pants on a woman would have been deemed way too tarty!

Inch by inch the full picture revealed itself, pieced together like a jigsaw. The next stage was the lingerie section of my auntie's Littlewoods catalogue. Studying the women in their bras and panties, I kept a finger in the hi-fi section so I could flick back instantly if anyone came in the room.

The Rubbish Shop, as we called it, was our salvation as sex-starved teenagers. The window display was bizarre: cracked saucers full of coat buttons; teapots and dented kettles; framed portraits enhanced by tea-cup rings. And, between the broken toasters and the Perry Como LPs, lay an untidy pile of creased and fusty magazines, *Health & Efficiency* among them.

The bell would ting-a-ling in the dusty silence at the back of the shop, and five minutes later an old hag with silver hair would shuffle out in her pom-pom slippers and a grimy nylon housecoat.

'I was, er, interested in the *Health & Efficiencies* in the window,' one of us would say. And she'd pull out a pile for us to peruse. Much too embarrassed to flick through the magazines in front of her, we'd just buy whatever covers attracted us.

'I'll have that. And that, and that. Oh, and that.'

The old hag made no judgements. She just ferreted out the magazines and rolled them up in an old newspaper, tucking in the ends and tying a bit of string round for extra security. Try getting that kind of service in W. H. Smith.

Health & Efficiency was a one-off. It was started in 1900 as a magazine for men and women who preferred life without clothes – nudists, naturists, sun worshippers, or whatever they called themselves. (Others would prefer perverts or oddballs.) You couldn't expect the English to understand.

Some people thought *H & E* was a dirty mag, but it wasn't. There were no raunchy letters, no smutty jokes, no women in kinky undies. Nakedness here was nothing to do with sex. These people thought they were part of a diaspora from the Garden of Eden, making do in the industrial West. I supported them, but they were much maligned, an easy butt for saucy seaside postcards. The magazine had two distinct classes of reader – genuine naturists, and the rest, males who just wanted to see naked women. Sod naturism! Who cared what the women were doing, or why, as long as they were naked. I liked *H & E* because the people in it were ordinary. Since they were not paid to be naked, it proved that nudity *per se* was nothing to be ashamed of.

It wasn't until the late sixties that I saw my first proper girlie mag.

Before they became nancified unisex salons, hairdressers were strictly men only, places to buy cigarettes, Durex and razor blades. The talk was of fishing and football. You could find a barber's on every other street, but as teenagers we always headed for Larry's, despite the queues. To keep customers amused, Larry kept a pile of soft-core girlie mags on the table – *Tit-Bits*, *Reveille*, *Spick* and *Span*. They were for the men, really, but no one ever objected to us lads browsing. They even watched us, smiling indulgently. But we didn't learn that much. We knew girls had boobs, but what else? Even in the 'swinging' sixties those lower regions were still out of sight. Yet all the curves led us there. Following the lines of breasts, hips, thighs, something in our genes told us something vital was missing. We had to know.

By the seventies the truth was revealed *in toto*. Young, daft and easily drunk, after last orders on Fridays we rolled round to the local Odeon for its late-night bill of tit-and-terror films like *The Vampire Lovers* and *Dracula A.D. 1972*. Jammed in the dusty red seats we laughed openly at plummy British actors trying to be Transylvanian inn-keepers, coaches belting through woods, invariably over-turning, one wheel left spinning for effect. Medieval crap. Nude scenes – that's what we wanted. Each glimpse of a wench's nipple or a barmaid's buttocks was greeted by a roar of appreciation. You had to take pot luck with these films, but as often as not we got a full-frontal: Ingrid Pitt stripping off and standing starkers in a tub full of virgin's blood.

The whole picture at last.

When the lights went up the manager did the choc-ice and Kia-Ora run himself in case we attacked the ice-cream girl.

But even before we'd learned to love women we'd learned to take the piss. At school someone brought in a book of rugby songs. An impromptu choir was convened in the 4C form room. Half a dozen pimply teenagers gathered round the paperback as if it was a profane hymn book. The chorus swelled up to yell out each fuck and prick. Their grins stretched further with each battering-ram smash against the gates of decency. I joined in, pretended to laugh, but the words stuck in my mouth, just like when I was nine and someone forced me to eat warm, rubbery broad beans. I gagged on each one as fear of being sick fought against fear of being punished.

I felt miserable and utterly disloyal. How could I let my mum down in this way? After what she'd gone through? After the love and the loyalty and the sacrifice? These songs disgusted me, celebrating the way men got women preg-nant and pissed off. Guilt? No way. These escapades were to be lauded. But being a single mum was no joke – how could anyone think so?

I didn't want to fall out with anyone, that was the trouble. Disagree and you ran the risk of being tagged queer or sissy. Why else would you protest? But I knew these songs were wrong. (I was too young to know, but I had allies.

Germaine Greer was already writing her book which would have these rugby-singing idiots on the run.) Back then I felt alone and too insignificant to raise my voice. Male propaganda was designed to make sure the little bastards accepted their tag and never protested.

Seeing a live naked woman was high on my agenda too, but I'd always assumed it would be a private thing, a joyful bedroom romp, just the two of us.

A mate's dad arranged the strip show for his son's 'coming-of-age' party. It came as part of an inclusive package: a blue comic and two strippers, fifty quid the lot. The comedian was bad enough (again we had to cheer every fuck or cunt), but what made me feel worse was the strippers. They weren't exactly class, but they were women and they were naked and I should have been wild with joy. And I might have been if I'd been on my own with them. But private enjoyment wasn't the point here.

The evening was nothing to do with love or even sex. I even doubted that any of the gawpers were turned on. If one of the strippers had gone round and started unbuttoning flies, she'd have had to winkle out their shrinking pricks twixt finger and thumb. It was sheer ritual, set up as an exercise in power and humiliation, an opportunity to show your allegiance to the male *esprit de corps*. I hated it. I wanted to run from the building, get those stupid drunken voices out of my head, forget the braying laughter.

The others lapped it up, quite literally. Ted, for instance, a mate who we suspected of kinkiness even then, thought his luck was in when one of the strippers sat on his knee. His tongue shot out as pink and steaming as a dog's when she held her boobs up to his face. Hard to tell who was humiliating who, but Ted didn't see it that way. Nor did the rest of them. They loved it. But couldn't they see she hated them? Did they really believe she was turned on by the presence of so many horny men, intoxicated by the gas-cloud of testosterone? Couldn't they see that given the chance she'd have preferred to spray them with gunfire?

Losing my identity in the drunken crowd was what frightened me. Having my 'me' dissolved in some poisonous solution of maleness. I wanted to think that when the stripper looked at me she'd know I was there against my will, just pretending. She'd know I was really a romantic. Some hope! All she saw, if she saw me at all, was one more drunken lout with a glassy-eyed stare.

The novelty of being a journalist didn't take long to wear off. Having survived Dennis's cruel tests about syntax, I'd passed my trial period without further comment and now felt established enough to take liberties. Despite frosty looks from Dennis, I happily allowed Colin to get me into the long lunch-hour habit. We'd typed up our readers' letters, captioned our pics and read the proofs – what was the point of rushing back?

'Full of character' would be a charitable way to describe Kilburn's pubs; 'cheerfully downmarket' far more accurate. The Priory Tavern, just across the yard from us, was Dennis's den. Over a cheese sandwich and half a lager, he brooded about why his pension scheme wasn't as good as the advertising director's or why Geoff, the studio manager, had been off with flu and sent in a sick note with a Brighton postmark.

Colin and I didn't give a shit about office politics. We wanted to get away, to talk about books and films, so we headed for the Memphis Belle on Kilburn High Road. This cavern of a tavern had a slowly decaying grandeur that was hard to resist. Alone in corners, bleary-eyed Irishmen sat listening to a jukebox full of mournful ballads from home. The barmaids were lovely brown-eyed waifs from Kerry and Limerick. Fixed up with work and digs in this sooty sector of NW6, they stood drying glasses, their prettiness reflected in half a dozen mirrors, shyly smiling at sozzled compliments from men in rusting suits.

Some days I stayed in the office and tackled the *Times*

crossword while Colin went off on a book-browsing binge. Colin loved books. Reading them, fondling them, sniffing them, even buying them. Sometimes he didn't even wait for lunchtime but just disappeared on the pretence of buying some cigarettes. After an hour Dennis would look at his watch and sigh.

'Go and see if he's in that bloody bookshop again!'

It was one of those trendy bookshops, packed with biographies of Peruvian revolutionaries, lesbian D-I-Y manuals and politically correct children's stories – all carefully vetted by the bearded owners for signs of frivolity. No Jeffrey Archer or Joanna Trollope here! Even its location was exquisitely right-on, grid-referenced between a greasy-spoon caff and a charity shop where mums from the nearby council flats clattered through the clothes rails in the hope of kitting-out their kids for next to nowt.

One day Colin went in with a list, which he handed to the earnest American girl on the desk. Her eyebrows twitched. Her ear-rings swivelled wildly as she jerked her head up to check him out. She had the kind of X-ray glare from which no secrets could be shielded. One glance and she knew you were the kind of person who chuckled at Carry On films and smacked their lips at the mention of lamb chops. She took an instant dislike to Colin.

'The Marquis de Sade?'

A couple of women in the Lesbian Lifestyle section turned to glare.

'*The Sex Life of the Foot and Shoe*? What kind of book is that?'

Colin hated being put on the spot. Bookshops were supposed to be havens. You could step out of the poisonous smog of the city and immediately lose yourself in Dostoevsky's Russia or Greene's Vietnam. Bookshops should be monkish retreats, oases of liberal thought – not while-u-wait interrogation parlours.

'It's a psycho-social investigation of pedic eroticism,' he explained patiently.

'Some kind of sexual fetish book, you mean? From a reputable publisher? Does it have an ISBN?'

Colin refused to justify his choices, especially for the pricked ears of the customers. He pointed out the salient details on the paper, left his phone number and asked to be notified when the books arrived.

Back at the office (after explaining his absence to Dennis) he launched into a furious tirade against mad feminists in glasses.

I like to think she'd been tailing him. Probably she simply checked out the phone number he'd given her. Whichever, the American girl had somehow sussed out what kind of place her least favourite customer worked in. When Colin returned a few days later she was ready for him. Not only had she not ordered the books, she wanted to make sure he knew why.

'It's our policy not to supply customers whose work involves them in the violation of feminist or socialist principles,' she explained in a humourless New Jersey drawl.

A few days later we arrived at work to be greeted by angry splashes of graffiti all over the front door.

FASCIST SEX PIGS!
RESPECT WOMEN! NO MORE EXPLOITING!
NAKEDNESS + VOYEURISM = RAPE!

We didn't need two guesses to connect it with the bookshop woman. London was full of oddball alliances and eccentric groups. As individuals they were merely nutters, two or three people meeting in a bedsit, but by using a name – Feminists Against Tyranny, Anti-Porn Alliance – they could give themselves phoney significance.

'Get it washed off, Geoff,' growled Russell Gay when he pulled up in his Mercedes.

It would take more than Fairy Liquid and a sponge to shift these opinions. Geoff had to beg petty cash and go out for some sandpaper. He spent hours rubbing. Unfortunately he eroded a large patch of paintwork at the same time. The door looked worse than ever.

The feminist–psychological reading hung over us like a shadow. Feminists drew dreadful parallels, frogmarching us to the edge of an old abandoned well and making us look down at the junk and sins and secrets, cluttered with dismembered bodies and the rag-doll victims of sex crimes. They allied Colin and me with Nazi doctors and the directors of snuff movies. Men hated women's bodies, they told us. Men wanted to own them, use them, abuse them. Victorian surgeons autopsied women's breasts and genitals on the slightest pretext, pickled them in jars like exotic lizards, kept them filed and ordered on high shelves in secret rooms. Science they called it. Men's science, a thin veneer for masturbatory fantasy.

I knew the theory. Part of me wanted to agree. Every time a rape or sex murder hit the headlines, I wondered if I was somehow involved, no matter how tenuously. Those men who wrote the queer and disturbing letters . . . maybe one of them had finally flown off the handle? Yet men have been raping and murdering for centuries, long before *Fiesta* and *Knave* appeared. Men need no lessons. Feminists made these simple links between magazines and rape and I was easy prey to guilt, but when I thought it out I wasn't so sure. Anyway, these women would never like me, no matter how much I agreed with them, not while I had a penis hanging between my legs. Desire was really hatred. Women gave us hard-ons, but we didn't love them for it, we hated them for making us lose control of ourselves.

At the end of the day, how could these feminists know? Putting themselves in a man's shoes was no more believable than a man pretending to be a woman. How could they, how dare they say that I hated women, that my desire for sex was a thinly veiled desire for power and enslavement?

I didn't know any hardline feminists, but even some of the women who knew me had similar ideas. They all subscribed to fashionable feminism and hated what I was doing. Yet they knew me too well, liked me too much, to hate me as a person. They knew I was not a devil, just an ordinary guy.

'How can you prostitute your IQ to bolster that awful stuff,' demanded Babs. (She was happily unaware that Guy had used her as a template for one of his stories, a would-be actress who begged a visiting meter reader for satisfaction.) 'Men like Russell Gay couldn't produce their sleazy mags if it wasn't for people like you.'

The unfairness enraged me. I'd always wanted a job with Amnesty or PEN. Even the RSPCA could have indulged my yearning to help. There simply weren't enough saintly jobs to go round. Some of us had to do the shit work, the dodgy stuff. And I hated how other people got away with it. I'd heard mums boasting about sons and daughters working at Barclays Bank or Lucas Aerospace or Philip Morris. They wore suits and had mortgages and solid careers. But no one was asking them any questions – about dodgy investments, weapons manufacture, selling fags to African kids. Their sins were hidden behind layers of respectability. By the time it reached their bank accounts, their money was suitably laundered and pressed.

Why should I be the sole scapegoat? I tried to argue, but feminism had got its teeth into pornography. No excuses were allowed.

I imagined being attacked in the street by militant feminists who would leave me in the gutter while they walked off waving my severed balls as a trophy!

But what was pornography? The opposition couldn't agree. From harmless naturist frolics to leather-dressed sado-masochism in secret cellars, they lumped everything together. By most standards British girlie mags were pretty mild. Feminists and zealots called it porn, but we were churning out seaside postcard stuff, more *Benny Hill* than the Marquis de Sade. Some punters may have yearned for hard sleaze, but no one would find any monkey business with donkeys on the top shelf of W. H. Smith! Like them,

I hated the splayed thighs shots in magazines like *Park Lane* and *Playbirds*. As a voyeur I was timid. I liked naked girls, but I didn't want to see them sprawled on the floor exposing their insides. I couldn't see any eroticism in that; those who wanted it were working to a different agenda.

I've never believed in the 'Slippery Slope Theory' – that men exposed to girlie mags all turn into rapists and molesters; that flipping a few pages of a soft-porn magazine soon leads to a secret life flashing at schoolgirls in the park, stealing knickers from unguarded clothes lines and renting heavy videos filmed in suburban dungeons. But this theory has always had an attractive simplicity:

'Did he read girlie magazines?'

Back in 1973, when the CID arrested a friend of ours for murder, it was the first question they asked us. Not having a girlfriend was suspicious, and so was the fact he might have read girlie mags and found naked girls appealing. There was no way to escape the catch-22 of suspicion. The only way to look innocent was to have a girlfriend and not read girlie mags – as if that were a perfect alibi.

Galaxy should have been used to nutty visitors, even if they didn't all splash the doors with paint. Part of Janice's job (and of course she resented it) was to sell copies of *Fiesta* and *Knave* to men who were too shy to buy them from the corner shop. Usually they just asked for the latest issue and Janice flung them a copy through her glass hatchway. If she could have taken their warm coins and limp banknotes with a pair of tweezers she would have.

Some meanies didn't want to part with money and treated the foyer like a reference library. They'd make out they were searching for a particular back number, forcing Janice to fetch half a dozen bound volumes for them to browse through. As they settled down for a free read, she'd watch with mounting disgust and impatience.

Not all Galaxy's visitors were punters. We attracted all kinds of semi-official hangers-on. They all had an excuse.

The local bobby who'd come to advise on security. The manager of the garage downstairs who'd come to give Russell his bill for a new clutch and stayed for two hours. We even had a fireman. He was only the boyfriend of one of the secretaries, but it was alarming to see him appear in his yellow helmet. Despite dozens of previous uneventful visits they still harboured hopes of catching us in the middle of some hanky-panky, catching sight of some model rushing nakedly from the dressing room to the toilet. Even the man from the electricity board must have relished his quarterly visits to read the meter. No doubt he wound his mates up with tall tales, the stunning birds he'd seen, the things he'd heard. And so the mythology grew, a web of lies and braggery.

Generally, Janice didn't mind entertaining these visitors. They were a refreshing change to pervy phone calls. I never let on, of course, to her or anyone else, but I always fancied Janice. I was madly jealous whenever her boyfriend came to collect her. She was going back with him, she'd unbutton the white blouse, drop the smart skirt, and he'd be there with his expectant smirk, as if it was all his. I hated him for having what I couldn't.

But despite the physical attraction, she didn't fit the rest of my criteria. She wasn't shy or well-spoken or bookish. She was a tough, flinty-tongued girl from north London; I was a daft romantic.

I couldn't even say I really liked her, could I? Not if I was being honest. This contradiction between idealism and desire was one that our readers had to deal with all the time. Hence, the letters from clerks in praise of women in black undies, the bit of 'rough', a woman they'd do anything to fuck, but who they couldn't trust to butter scones properly. What a dilemma they faced, trying to reconcile their social position and the insistent urges of their balls. As a socialist, I liked to think it was evolution's way of trying to buck the class system.

*   *   *

Our would-be models weren't all desperate. Some of them, intoxicated by their own perfume, were as bright as canaries, a-twitter with all kinds of daydreams.

Suzy, for instance. She had no CSEs, but God had compensated by blessing her with blonde curls, blue eyes and impossibly pointed tits. She knew she was lovely and she was determined to make the most of herself. She'd made herself up for the occasion and couldn't resist a bitch at the girl who'd passed her on the way out to pin-up oblivion.

'My dad's got bigger tits than her!' She flicked through the test Polaroids that Geoff had left unguarded on the chair. 'Four cans of Carlsberg every night, that'll do the trick. Give her tits a bit of bounce. Just like my dad!'

'Some men like small ones,' Pam said, in the girl's defence. She'd been sneering at the no-hoper herself ten minutes ago, but no way would she let snooty bitches like Suzy take the piss out of some poor housewife.

'Some men like little boys as well.' Unconcerned about privacy, Suzy stood at the changing-room curtain and stripped with complete lack of shyness. She unhooked her bra, flung it over the back of the chair and grinned at Geoff. 'Real men like a decent pair of boobs, don't they?'

Geoff coughed diplomatically and busied himself with the light meter.

Suzy was a bitch, but she was also a winner. Totally at ease, she had that drop-dead self-assurance that men find such a turn-on. Lucky lass, to have been given that power over the male sex. There was no rhyme or reason in it, justice had never figured in the allocation of talent. She was just a kid from a council estate, but she could go far.

She had it planned. *Fiesta* today, *Penthouse* next month, and Hollywood next year. Well, maybe not Hollywood. But she'd make herself known. She'd be wanted by every man in the country. And she knew the ones to pick – a rock star here, a Formula One driver there, a company chairman, anyone who got flashed by the paparazzi, anyone who could help get her face in the paper.

She'd done her homework too. Every detail of famous models' income was filed away in her scheming brain.

'Ten grand a shoot, they can get,' Suzy told us. 'Five grand just for opening a bloody Tesco's shop. Seven if it's one of their out-of-town superstores.'

You could see the pound signs in her eyes as she totted up her fantasy bank balance. I had a sneaking admiration for her. Back home I'd seen too many pretty girls throw themselves away by getting hitched to some fat bozo. ('What the hell is she going out with that arsehole for?' we often wondered out loud, though not within earshot of said arsehole.)

We'd always believed in some kind of system. Beautiful girls went with handsome blokes. Average girls settled for average men. And fat spotty bastards got left with greasy-haired shrews. Logical, fair, Darwinian, we hated to see it thwarted. To cheat it meant big trouble. How could a pretty lass be smitten by a creep? We could see what lay ahead, why couldn't she? Once the sweet talk was done with she'd be up the stick, and hooked like a gaping trout. From then on she'd be a doormat, ironing shirts, feeding babies, hoovering dust, while Dickhead was at the pub chucking lager down his neck. In an alarmingly short period she'd be well down the road to fatness and tranquillizers.

Wasn't Suzy right, then? Wasn't it better to use your good looks to make some money instead of giving yourself away to some idiot? Sure, men just like him were going to wank over your pictures, but that was only virtual reality. Let 'em wank, at least you were free and had money in the bank.

Suzy peeled off her black panties and flopped down on the chesterfield, shamelessly displaying a patch of auburn hair that someone (a helpful boyfriend?) had clipped into a heart shape.

'You've got to make an effort, haven't you?' she said, noting Geoff's surprise. She tickled the hairs with a crimson fingernail and sniggered filthily.

Test-shots aren't intended to be glamorous, just a rough guide that allows editors to pore over profiles and vital statistics. But Suzy was determined to make the session into a big occasion. She had perfected the pouts and the come-hither expressions. They seemed quite natural too. Even in the playground she'd probably been a coquette.

Dennis was pleased with her anyway. He knew a winner when he saw one. Immediately he phoned Jim Stone, *Fiesta*'s resident lensman, to come and have a look.

Suzy would never make the millions she craved. Tesco's would never invite her to open a superstore. But she'd certainly be asked back to do a full session with Jim. She'd be delighted. Less pleased when she found out, after eventually appearing in *Fiesta*, that £150 was a more likely pay-off than £2000.

Friday was studio day, with Jim Stone on the Hasselblad, Geoff busily engaged with set construction and lighting, and Dennis as 'director'. Sometimes he rang me on the internal phone and summoned me in, just to make some minor query. It looked suspiciously like another test, designed to see if I could keep my cool in the presence of real naked women, live and kicking and walking about with casual indifference to all the males. I wasn't embarrassed, but neither did I want to be cast as an ogler, so I never looked long enough to risk stimulation. My only thoughts were about how unfair it was for Jim Stone and Geoff to enjoy such pleasant working conditions.

Galaxy's regular models, at first glance, looked no different to the wannabes. They'd simply grasped the notion of what *Fiesta*'s readers wanted, practising and perfecting all the superficial tricks – the pout, the lip-licking, the hair preening – which were accepted code for a woman with nymphomanic leanings. Under Dennis's direction, they simply had to switch on one or more of the above. Consummate models could easily adopt the pleading 'fuck me, big boy' look or the wide-eyed shock that said: I've never seen such a big one before!

73

Professional technique – it was nothing more than that, a small repertoire of masks and mimes. Rather than I want you now, hard inside me, their thoughts were more likely to be along the lines of, It's bloody chilly in here, or, I hope they've got that Marks and Spencer quiche for lunch.

I found it hard to believe that men would fall for it. They weren't that gullible, were they? But, if they were, who was exploiting whom? And why did we need to think about exploitation at all? Some men wanted to look, and since it paid their rent, some girls willingly obliged, a simple arrangement that dated back to doctors and nurses games. Some feminists despise the men who look, and cast the girls as victims of an economic conspiracy. Sure, few women would do it if they didn't need the money; but the same can be said for men who join the army. The models I encountered rarely thought of themselves as the victims their right-on sisters wanted them to be. They were, if not happy with the work, at least not miserable. It wasn't brilliant money, but it was easy money and earned in a good-humoured atmosphere. They certainly preferred it to clattering the keys of a typewriter for eight hours a day. For other women to think on the models' behalf was to patronize them.

But it's true that if the models didn't make much money, Galaxy certainly did. After a set would eventually appear in *Fiesta*, the company garnered a healthy income from syndicating the pictures around the world. Nakedness was a universal language. Possibly unbeknown to them, these girls were being ogled in America, Belgium or even India.

'Don't you fancy getting on the photography side of it?' Tone asked me one day.

'How do them blokes handle it?' Phil wanted to know. 'Surrounded by naked women all day long—'

'Never be short of a fucking screw,' agreed Tone.

Jim Stone stumbled into photography as clumsily as I did into journalism. Until a couple of years previously he'd been a wrestler. But he'd got fed up. What kind of life was it, being mangled and sat on by men with smelly crotches and names like Bonebreaker Smith and Jeff 'Hell Hound' Simpkins? Why he chose photography, no one could say, but they guessed it might have been something to do with naked women.

It would be surprising if it wasn't. New girls are especially vulnerable. Starkers, alone, a good photographer puts them at ease, makes them feel good about doing it, whispers encouragement, drops a timely compliment. This is the man who can turn them from shop girl into a cover girl. It's a saintly photographer who doesn't sometimes take advantage.

The fact he spent his working day in the company of naked women only made us dislike him. We could hardly blame him for that! And since he enjoyed Dennis's grudging patronage, he had a charmed life. He cheerfully did whatever Dennis told him to do and gave him no backchat about artistic independence.

Not all of the photography was done in-house. We relied on freelances. Weary looking photographers were always begging an audience with Dennis. He enjoyed the power, making them stand by nervously while he pored over their sheets of trannies with his spy-glass.

I'd only been joking. Perhaps I'd had a pint too many, but I told Tone and Phil, if they fancied their chances, *Fiesta* was always looking for fresh photographers and models. If Jim could make a living from it it couldn't be that difficult to do, and some of those freelances earned even more. But it wasn't the money that made Tone and Phil's eyes roll, more the idea of being with naked women all day long.

'I've got a camera,' said Phil.

The next day he brought it along to the pub. He wanted my opinion on it, as if a good camera was all that mattered. And it wasn't even a good one.

'No, you'd need a lot more than an Instamatic,' I said.

'It's got a flash,' he added desperately. He looked so

disappointed. For one crazy moment he thought this camera was like some magical machine that would somehow change his life.

'You could always do some Readers' Wives and send them in,' I suggested in an effort to sooth his disappointment.

They looked around the pub in anticipation. A few women sat at the bar sipping their G & Ts. The idea of approaching them and asking them to pose naked was frightening.

Every month, when the pin-ups had been picked, I had to do half a dozen 'girlie blurbs'. Girlie mags paid lip service to the importance of personality, but the only personality these girls had was the one invented for them by Colin and me. The blurbs were pure fiction, and nonsensical fiction at that. Oddly enough, after all the scepticism I got about the letters, the readers seemed to believe the bullshit. People like Tone and Phil happily believed the crap I rattled off:

> Gorgeous 22-year-old Tracey has just got her
> Economics degree from Cambridge. Yep, she's
> a smart lass. Apparently the Cambridge lads
> like a bit of a punt during the summer and
> Tracey's had more than a few invites from men
> with a long pole. 'I love laying back and watch-
> ing the guys do all the work. Some of them are
> really handy with their poles. Then we stop off
> in a meadow somewhere and I give them a bite
> to eat in return for their hard work . . .'

Sometimes it came easily. A punt was an easy prop to spin a yarn around and the pole an obvious target for euphemism. And some pictures featured a nippy sports car or a beach scene. But occasionally all the art room threw at us was a naked woman and a settee. No props, no personality, nothing. In that event, there were all kinds of things to fall back on. The foreign angle was always reliable – foreign girls, creaking euphemisms, hopeless clichés:

> 'We German girls love our sausages long and
> meaty. After a day's modelling work I always
> look forward to getting home. Hans, my boy-
> friend, always has a steaming bratwurst ready
> for my supper. You should see me tucking into
> it. I really appreciate Hans' skills, in the kitchen
> and the bedroom.'
> Helga certainly knows her sausages, guys!
> Wouldn't you love the chance to introduce her
> to the taste of a British porker!?

The words we put into their mouths, the wishful thoughts of every reader:

> 'I like a man to be a man,' says Tracey. 'Then
> I'll do anything for him.' She runs her pink and
> very flexible tongue across her lips. 'And I
> mean anything . . .'

Needless to say Colin and I both hated it. But it became automatic. I'd just dream up blurbs in my idle hours, leaving out specific references to hair colour or boob size, then marry them up to whatever pictures were tossed on my desk.

The art room was an enclave all of its own, protected by two viciously sprung doors, one at each side. With its draw-ing boards and intense lighting it had a slightly spooky sci-fi feel, like the inside of some alien spaceship. Their allegiance to art, even in its pornographic mode, made these graphic cats all too superior. Rick and Tony and Jenny acted as though they were in on some big secret – the secret of cool. I could never enter the art room without thinking someone was sneering at the style of my shoes or the cut of my shirt. The rest of us could see them through the glass, hear their laughter, but it was a private world in there.

Dennis was doubly estranged because of his age. He wanted to exert discipline, but he knew it was futile. The art room were a law unto themselves.

They made up rules as they went along. I'd comment that such and such a girl was quite nice looking, and they'd look at me with pity. Post-modern was the buzz word. Beauty and perfection were old hat and politically suspect. It was the freaks you had to admire, the Readers' Wives acting kittenish against a background of mock-tasteful lounge furniture and bedrooms with Laura Ashley curtains.

We were never sexually distracted by our work. It would have been an impossible job if we'd had to sit there with a constant erection or have to rush off to the toilet every half an hour to let off steam with a wank!

In any case, I rarely saw anyone in *Fiesta*'s pages to turn me on. Our typical model (definition: 'person or thing proposed for imitation, an ideal standard') bore little resemblance to the kind of woman I fancied. My taste for girls with short elfin hairstyles led some people to speculate on whether I was a latent homosexual. When I said I liked girls in simple white blouses the consensus was I must be a fancier of schoolgirls. And to say I hated Page Three girls was the worst of all. I was obviously a bit of a wimp. Apart from mentioning my quirks to Guy, I kept quiet about it. At least he was individual enough to understand that these preferences were not secret signals. After all, he had a thing about girls in army camouflage jackets, but I never drew any conclusions from that.

Uniforms figured large in reader fantasies: policewomen, traffic wardens, Wrens, lady judges, nurses, prison warders. These women had power or status, but the magazines, of course, stripped them of it, literally. Policewomen and traffic wardens, unbuckled and unbuttoned, are women who desperately need a man. Even the guerrilla licking the barrel of her Kalashnikov is only making do until the right man comes along to satisfy her.

Salvation Army girls, schoolgirls and nuns were banned – not because of a lack of fans, but because religion and under-age stuff were against the guidelines. Not that the nuns would ever look holy, the schoolgirls under twenty or the sets particularly convincing – it was the thought that was *verboten*.

A monthly ritual was the reading of the sales reports, little blue-covered booklets, in which sales reps, wholesalers and selected newsagents were invited to give their professional opinions on each issue of *Fiesta* and *Knave*:

> This month's cover is a winner! Dionne is always a firm favourite with customers. The shiny pink lipstick was a great idea – one glance and that's another sale! Contentwise, the black stilettos set was widely regarded as first-class, as was this month's jokes page. Readers' Wives, however, are often uneven and can attract sarcastic remarks! (newsagent)

> Somerset retail outlets report disappointing sales for February's issue, up to 4 per cent down on January. The navy blue title is a turn-off. Redheads are also unpopular. One of my clients says that his customers perceive them as spiteful rather than sexy. However, the blonde on pages 44–49 is more what the customer is looking for. (regional rep)

> Customers are very much against the barcodes appearing across a cover girl's naked parts. Now the price has increased, perhaps it would be time to make the typeface smaller? (regional rep)

Though Dennis demanded we listen seriously, few of us did. With bylines like James of Manchester & N.West, and Geoff, South Wales, these comments contained uncanny echoes of our readers' letters. But for these collar-and-tie chaps in their company Volvos, *Fiesta* and *Knave* were simply products, of no more interest than *Yachting Monthly* and *Railway World*. Being asked for their opinions was part of their job.

Guy and I had come to the end of an era. I'd got so involved with Elaine that we'd decided to get our own place. It was only across the road, but it was a quantum leap in many ways. It meant no more freedom for me. It wasn't just the rent that was worrying Guy: he couldn't believe that I'd give up all that freedom, my own space, my own privacy. But despite Guy's dire warnings, I walked into the set-up with a happy heart.

The set-up at my new place was a microcosm of Belsize Park life. The six first-floor bedsits all housed different lifestyles in uneasy adjacency. Some of the 'rooms' were original rooms which had been divided in half with hardboard partitions.

'I can hear every single thing you and Elaine do,' Mimi said sourly, referring to a life under siege on the other side of the partition. 'All that gasping,' she added.

'That's Elaine . . . she's a bit asthmatic,' I said weakly.

But we weren't the only ones up to hanky-panky. Keith, the wanking signalman, was always pestering me for free copies of *Fiesta*. He must have had the same problem with his co-partitioners, Yusif and Melanie. And from what we heard, Yusif fancied a slap more than a tickle.

In the old days there'd often been weeks on end when I'd never had sex or seen anyone naked. Even when I had a date there was always an element of doubt as to whether we'd do it or not. Now I was in the presence of nudity every night. Elaine ran in from the bath naked. We dressed and undressed in each other's presence, spent our nights with our skins pressed together. Until then nudity had always been a big treat, but now, day and night, it quickly became part of everyday life, not the green light for fucking.

I had to learn to bracket off the private pleasures of nudity from nudity at work, nudity at home for no special reason.

Sometimes a mighty dread seized my troubled mind: what if one day naked females lost their novelty altogether ... I remembered stories I'd heard about impotent men: how could anyone not get a hard-on at the sight of a naked woman? What if that happened to me?

Maybe I wasn't ready for a proper grown-up relationship. I loved Elaine, but when it came to it, I didn't like sharing a bed. Beds were private spaces, places for listening to Tony Hancock on headphones, sniggering in the dark without feeling daft. I didn't mind the feel of a woman next to me, but I felt guilty for not paying attention. We'd built up this big mythology about the bed. You couldn't mention the word without someone winking or inventing a rumour. But really, they were for sleeping in. They didn't have to be synonymous with sex, did they?

4 Readers' Wives

We called it 'The Two Week Live-In'. Twenty-five years or so later, the memory still raises a laugh. Pete's parents had gone on holiday and a bunch of us moved in for the duration. The menu was crazy: Smash, beans, incinerated burgers, fried eggs in currant buns, washed down with a choice of stewed tea or warm Coke. The valves of the fifties stereogram glowed red hot and sizzled as they tried to cope with the sonic overload of *Led Zeppelin II*.

A love-in, that's what it should have been, of course. But none of the girls we knew was willing to play along. They were always telling us how faithfully they'd serve the hunky one out of Free, but, unsurprisingly, they preferred to stay in and watch *Coronation Street* rather than service a bunch of greasy youths in tie-dyed T-shirts. Robert Plant may have got someone to squeeze his lemon, but for us 'Got A Whole Lotta Love' was no more than a cruel irony.

So, for want of anything better, we got some cans in and settled down for a flick through Pete's carpet-walloping hi-rise collection of *Mayfair*s and *Penthouse*s.

Blonde, blue-eyed, with long legs and perfectly poised 34Bs, the dolly bird still ruled. All London girls of course (from a postal district that was part Chelsea, part Kensington and part Mayfair), for no one associated beauty and sex appeal with plebeian townships like Stoke or Doncaster. Redneck Midlanders like us would never meet stunners like this. But, for the price of a mag we could dream of being their window cleaners. We'd catch them unawares, stepping out of the shower, lounging on a sofa in unbuttoned blouses, their fannies veiled in curls of purest gold. Caroline, Annabel, Penelope, Joanna – even their names smelled of Chanel.

Yet we were never alone. An unseen third party always lurked off-camera. James Bond, Simon Templar, Jason King, some smooth bastard shaking a cocktail, drawing on a Rothmans and smirking. Those buttons hadn't been slipped loose for our benefit, it wasn't us they purred for. Our clumsy chat-ups – 'Ayup, duck, fancy a Cherry B?' – would only make them smile. We had neither the dosh nor the elocution to compete. Bloody unfair! The throb against our palms told us we were just as capable of satisfying, but a twist of demography had fated us to be gooseberries.

But one of us at least had got a steady. Rick had been 'courting' Jenny for three months, virtually a marriage in teenage terms. They'd gone as far as they could in a vertical position – snogging at the bus stop, fingering each other in shop doorways – so, for them, the main draw of the live-in was the chance of an undisturbed shag.

As soon as they'd gone upstairs we went into action. The symbolism was exquisite. As Jenny coaxed Rick to readiness, we were in the yard seeing to an erection of our own, silently extending a ladder up to the adjacent bathroom. The joke was to burst in on them and get a souvenir snapshot, but by the time Bozz got to the windowsill they'd finished! Just as he climbed into the bathroom in walked Jenny, naked except for a smile. There was a flash, a scream, and before she had the chance to grab some cover, Bozz had scrambled back down into the yard.

Rick came storming down the stairs, but Bozz was already astride his bike. Dodging a wallop, he whizzed down the 1-in-45 driveway, did a 90° skid in the gutter, and pedalled furiously in the direction of home. The full-frontal snap was developed that same evening (Bozz was a science swot and had his own dark room) and passed around the gang. Rick was furious.

'Everybody's seen my bird,' he wailed.

The way he went on about it anyone would think we'd

gatecrashed the room and re-enacted some nasty *Straw Dogs* style gang bang. We'd seen Jenny's belly button on a day trip to Rhyl and he'd been touchy enough about that (remarking, 'Want a photograph or summat?'), but a full-frontal?

'It's not fucking right . . .'

A woman's nudity was sacrosanct. It wasn't just hers, it belonged to her fella too. He had exclusive viewing rights. More than jealousy, it involved pagan superstition: if another man caught so much as a glimpse the woman's mystique was destroyed. We all knew now how big Jenny's boobs were and that she wasn't a natural blonde.

Oddly enough, Jenny wasn't as upset as Rick. She made out she was, but only to be loyal. Once over the shock (and the temporary blindness) she found our interest flattering. And pathetic. What sexy power games she could play on us if she chose to. None of us would admit it, but the joke had backfired. Now we'd seen the photo there wasn't one of us who wouldn't have swapped places with Rick. We all wanted a copy, but Bozz reckoned he'd run out of paper.

A few years later the whole morality got turned on its head. By the mid-seventies hundreds of men had sloped arms, stood down the guard. The Polaroid camera had just been introduced and nudie snaps of wives and girlfriends started arriving at mags like *Fiesta*.

Ever since man first twiddled with a camera he's begged women to get their knickers off. Even in the brothels of Paris in the 1860s it was going on (house tariff: 20 francs for full sex, 15 francs for a hand-job, and 10 francs for a souvenir snapshot). A hundred and twenty years later nothing much had changed. Anyone with a Barclaycard could stroll into Dixons and come out fully equipped for home-made pornography:

Please find enclosed twelve photographs of my delicious wife, Linda. I know your readers will

go mad when they see her long shapely legs
and her suckable nipples.
PS. Please ensure that the payment cheque is
made out in my name as the photographer.

The wives seemed willing enough. Some played it brassy,
some kittenish, but they looked as if they were having a
good old laugh. One or two averted their faces, but the rest
played to the camera. Rather than feeling exploited, they
seemed to like the idea of being admired by thousands of
men. Readers' Wives was a chance for every woman, young
or old, pretty-pretty or pretty ugly, to sample the peculiar
frisson of posing nude.

No one can be sure now who first had the idea, but when
Readers' Wives became an institution, everyone fought for
the credit of having started it. Yet it was hardly intentional.
When that first amateur shot arrived, I'm sure they all had
a good laugh about it. The nerve of these punters! Still, it'd
fill a gap. They'd stick her on the letters pages, along with
the other readers' pics. Like the kinky vegetables, this
housewife was a novelty item. A bit of make-up might have
helped, and they could have moved that Tesco bag off the
settee, but she wasn't bad looking.

What no one expected was fan mail. Just a letter or two
at first, but enough to set them thinking. When another
wife from the sticks got the thumbs-up Russell Gay realized
they were on to something. Readers' Wives, far from being
ironic amusements, were hot stuff:

I must confess to being wildly excited by Tina
of Norwich . . .

Pat D. is the most shapely and delightfully
mature lady I've seen for years. I can't resist
looking at her pictures again and again.

I'm not a dirty old man, I'm happily married
with two lovely children. But I'm captivated by

Maureen of Leeds. I'd give a million to spend
an hour or two with her . . .

Tina, Pat, Maureen, Sue, Janet, Gail; the wind of change
was blowing, wafting away the scent of Chanel, replacing it
with the whiff of Charlie and Stowaway (with background
notes of lavender air freshener and wet rusks).

Was it a spontaneous social phenomenon? A backlash
against women's lib? Some might have called it a kind of
sexual democracy. Or were men reasserting their rights,
trading pics of their wives' boobs like kids swapping
bubblegum cards? Money wasn't the draw (just a couple
of quid was the payment then) so it had to be something
else. A kind of proxy prickteasing: you could look, but you
couldn't touch. But it was more than showing off. These
husbands knew what men were like, knew quite well that
Fiesta readers would be pushing off their Y-Fronts and
wanking over their wives. They even wrote and told us
how turned on they were by the idea:

Thanks for publishing the pics of my wife,
Jean, in August's *Fiesta*. She was really turned
on to think of a load of horny guys looking at
her naked and slowly wanking themselves to
orgasm. That night we had the best fuck we'd
had for years.

By the time I started at *Fiesta*, Readers' Wives was well
established. Every post brought more and there was a huge
backlog. Choosing each month's selection wasn't one of my
jobs – an art room selection was approved by Dennis – but
I did get to see them, if only for the simple task of thinking
up pseudonyms. I looked forward to it. Readers' Wives
gave me a chance to recapture part of my youth. That domestic backdrop was a key factor: the bedroom, the crumpled
sheets, the drawn curtains, the wife in her undies, sex in
the afternoon . . .

86

Young, randy, with flexible morals, I'd had no qualms about getting mixed up with a housewife. Rather, it gave me a huge buzz. Having an affair with another man's wife didn't half enhance my standing. My last girlfriend had been a skinny fifteen-year-old, and though she was on for some heavy petting, my mates jeered me as a cradle snatcher. They could hardly accuse me of that now I was shagging another man's wife. Julie had made the first move, but I grabbed the glory. Amoral, risky, grown up, it fitted in with every heroic criterion.

It was dangerous fun, waiting at the corner till he'd gone to work, then strolling in as cocky as you like. Forbidden fruit! I'd gone face down in a ripe melon and come up laughing like a drunkard.

It all blew up of course. What followed was a concerted campaign by in-laws and do-gooders – just what young lovers need to give their romance an edge. Julie's hubby was a mild-mannered pacifist who didn't hold with fisticuffs. If he had he'd have put me to flight in minutes. Instead he was a ridiculous diplomat, bribing me to stay away while he tried to patch up his marriage. I took his money and made empty promises. I spent it on fags and beer and still went round to see Julie.

Ten years on, those memories were fixed in amber. I still remembered the dry-mouthed heart-racing moment when she locked the bedroom door, slipped off her blouse, stepped out of her pants. Nothing would ever match that, but in those Readers' Wives backdrops I lived it all again.

Fiesta's rivals sneered at the Readers' Wives. It scared them to think they might not be the arbiters of male taste they fancied themselves as. Mags like *Mayfair* and *Men Only* aspired for a place on that global top shelf alongside *Penthouse* and *Playboy*. They were in airport bookstalls, an international brand like Rothmans King Size and Canadian Club. The parochial and the plain was out. How could jetsetting businessmen and oil barons relate to housewives from Hull and Pwllheli? Men wanted class, not a bunch of factory girls and grandmas.

But did they?

The girlie-mag business was built on a dodgy premise: that there was an absolute scale of values. The morons who watched *Miss World* were led to believe that, despite the statistical improbability, the organizers had vetted the world's 1500 million women and found the thirty most beautiful. Bullshit! You could go into town and find twenty equally sexy women: on the checkout at Tesco's, behind the counter at Boots, tapping away on the town's typewriters.

Readers' Wives was the first challenge to all that. *Mayfair* and *Men Only* were full of stunners, but men knew they were, after all, professionals. They took their clothes off for money. What men really wanted to see was that girl in Tesco's, the wife of the bloke next door, the best mate's girlfriend. Readers' Wives had Marks and Spencer bras and real-life panties. This was real womanhood, worlds away from the sizzling promises of lacy bras and knickers as flimsy as cobwebs. Their pubes hadn't been prettied and perfumed, they were untamed and gave off an exciting feral fragrance. Some of them had had children and their nipples were stubby and brown and less than precious. Men felt comfortable in their company.

Liking dolly birds had always been half bravado. But now those posh-looking gals had escaped their West End playpens, become new women; smart blondes with their own ideas and their own chequebooks. Suddenly they were frightening, powerful, hungry. *Fiesta* readers wanted women back in their rightful place – the bedroom, the lounge, halfway up the stairs.

Not everyone made it. Even Readers' Wives had to draw the line somewhere. Britain may have harboured thousands of unsung pin-ups, but some would have been better advised to avoid the humiliation. There they all were, jostled together in a gloomy hen-party at the bottom of a giant Jiffy bag marked 'Doubtful': frights, sights, scarecrows, boilers, dogs and gargoyles. Some of them were positively medieval, bow-legged spindleshanks, indoor whales bursting out of scarlet lingerie. Girlfriends, wives, mothers and aunties, they must have been loved by someone. But still, to be rejected by Readers' Wives must have been the ultimate downer.

And – *quelle surprise* – who was the first (and only) one of our gang to go in for taking bedroom snaps? Only Rick. Babysitting for him a few years later, we stumbled on a clutch of Polaroids stuffed down the side of some sofa cushions. Jenny we'd seen already, though she looked a touch more relaxed in these pics. But why was Rick taking snaps of his own willy?

When Colin took over the editorship of *Video World*, Dennis asked me if I'd like to take charge of *Knave*. My own magazine – a chance thousands would jump at. I pretended to think it over, for politeness' sake, but I knew I'd turn it down. An editor had to show dedication, commitment and ambition. And I couldn't. So far I'd had an easy ride. Playing the humble hack – head down over the proofs, busily typing copy – as long as I kept to the schedules and caused no fuck-ups it was easy to hide my lack of enthusiasm. I was happy to follow orders – that way I could wriggle out of much of the blame.

And editorship looked too much like hard work. Dennis's chain-smoking was a dead give-away. I'd heard him arguing with Russell Gay, I'd seen him sweating over books, trying to balance the monthly budget. He'd taken on so much work that even his secretary needed a secretary, a timid West Indian girl who fidgeted endlessly in her chair. When she landed the task of labelling and recording the Readers' Wives pictures she went rigid, like a rabbit caught in a car's headlights. Sweet and unworldly, it was hard not to feel sorry for her. As a single mum, she desperately needed the money, but she obviously wished the Job Centre had sent her somewhere else.

Dennis had to advertise to fill the *Knave* jobs. Finding an editor was easy enough, but assistant editors were always more difficult somehow.

Clive was ex-public school and a nervous wreck. He seemed an unlikely choice. Couldn't the City have found a quiet place for him? If he insisted on journalism, surely his father had some old pals on *The Times* who'd oblige? Obviously not. *Knave* seemed to suit him just right.

But why should I think the titillation trade had a type? Porn appealed across all classes, so why shouldn't its creators be just as diverse? God, surely I couldn't be thinking that I was fit for porn while Clive's plummy vowels qualified him for something better? Perhaps, like me, he lacked qualifications and this was the first door that opened. Anyway, he entered into the work with gusto. If his copy was run-of-the-mill, it wasn't through lack of enthusiasm. He knew just as many dirty words as the rest of us. A public-school education certainly hadn't protected him from the world of male bravado, its lingua franca of pricks and cunts and pumping spunk.

Unlike Colin's desk, with its tottering piles of books and its film of French fag ash, and mine with its horrific backlog of readers' letters, Clive's desk was run with hygienic efficiency. Any papers that were not active were neatly filed away in a green filing cabinet (and since no one else bothered with them he had all four drawers to himself). In idle moments he polished the keys on his typewriter and picked out fluff with a bent paperclip. We all made typing mistakes, but while Colin and I sloshed on Tipp-Ex with the whistling carelessness of men whitewashing a wall, Clive stippled his mistakes away with the delicate brush strokes of an impressionist.

Every night before leaving, he arranged his desk with military precision. Ruler perfectly aligned with the edge of the desk; three freshly sharpened pencils; paperclips; eraser. My mum had brought me up to be neat – so why did I hate to see it in anyone else? Jealousy maybe, or maybe I just hated to see how prissy it looked. Whatever, I was determined to sabotage it.

At first he blamed the cleaners, but that wasn't good enough for me. I wanted him to know. Every time I walked past his desk I nudged his ruler out of place. While he was in the toilet I tightened the cap on his Tipp-Ex with a pair of pliers. I spent hours daisy-chaining all his paperclips. The *coup de grâce* was buying a small fish from Sainsbury's and putting it in the folder he'd neatly labelled 'For Possible Inclusion In *Knave* Xmas Special'.

The British are so bound up with their beds that any other bonking location is automatic proof of a wild life and sexual adventure:

> . . . after a couple of drinks we ended up snog-
> ging and I asked her if she wanted to come
> back to my place. She was so worked up she
> couldn't wait. Soon as we got on the bus she
> had her hand inside my jeans and started play-
> ing with my prick. When the two women got
> off she flung off her knickers and sat astride
> me for a shag . . .

People loved these tales of public shagging and alfresco sex, but they took them with a large pinch of salt. Yet it wasn't so incredible, was it? Elaine and I had it off on Hampstead Heath, patting down a bed of grass for ourselves between the trees. All went well until we'd finished. Just as I was putting my pants back on, a wire-haired mongrel rustled through the undergrowth and stood beady eyed as Elaine hurried to get dressed, all fingers and thumbs with her bra. Then the dog's owner appeared. Far from being thrilled he glared at us as if we were exposing his beloved pooch to moral danger. He gave Elaine's wobbling breasts a look of deep contempt, called his dog to heel and stomped off.

Working at *Fiesta* was to blame – or so I tried to kid myself. But what if I'd always been kinky, if *Fiesta* was just me sliding into a ready-made niche? Odd memories kept bobbing back up. I'd had sex on a roof in Baker Street. That wasn't so odd, surely? But what about that time with Julie in an allotment shed, only yards from where old guys were mulching up their pea crops? What if the codger whose shed it was had come to get his rake? And the shed was only a flimsy structure – what if our energetic bonking had sent it crashing to the ground?

Worse; there was that train journey to Birmingham when Shirley D. had actually got my prick out of my trousers and was idly working it up and down. What was that all about – teenage lust, a silly dare, a challenge to British Rail's authority? It could easily have ended up as a court case. And what was I thinking of when my mates were at the next table?

Surely I should have grown out of that sniggering and bravado stage. Despite these occasional pranks, I felt quite domesticated. Yet when Tone asked one day, 'You ever done that three-in-a-bed stuff?' I couldn't resist saying yes.

Three in a bed? Yes, I'd experienced it, but I wasn't going to give Tone and Phil the details – especially as the third party in question was a dog.

I'd been going out with Carole before I met Elaine, but I enjoyed sex with her so much I couldn't help but carry on seeing her occasionally. About once every two months we'd meet up for a trip to the cinema, then go back to her place in Balham. Elaine wasn't too pleased, but she grudgingly allowed it since there was no chance of Carole and me getting serious.

Carole's dog wasn't an active participant, thank God. He only climbed in alongside us when we'd finished having sex. Carole reckoned he was highly strung and needed to keep an eye on her. But his presence unsettled me. If there's such a thing as canine voyeurism, this was an example. I always dreaded he'd jump up and start licking my unprotected arse as I neared my climax. Or worse; that I didn't realize who was doing it and found it a turn-on.

Apart from this bi-monthly trip to Balham, I considered myself quite domesticated. Even faithful. They were two adjectives I'd never be able to apply to Guy. Occasionally he had a romance that lasted weeks instead of days, and I thought he might have finally settled down. But three months seemed to be his limit. If he had settled down, maybe I'd have been happy with my lot. Seeing him with a different girl every other week just reminded me of the freedom I'd surrendered. I tried to fool myself by sneering at his promiscuity, telling him that he was missing out on the joys of a steady relationship. He dismissed my evangelism out of hand. He knew that, like most preachers, I was a liar and a hypocrite.

I loved Elaine and I wanted to make a go of it. But part of me was still a wanderer. I tried so hard not to think unfaithful thoughts. It was possible in winter, because it was cold and dark and everyone was well wrapped up. But come spring and summer, the time of short skirts and summer dresses and crisp white blouses, my heart ached with desire. I blamed it on the chemicals, the procreation programme that had been hard-wired into my brain.

'I Confess' was the monthly task I dreaded most. Three tales, all a thousand words long and from a female point of view. The angle was men boast, women confess – hardly a subtle distinction. We and the public were their priests, one ear cocked for juicy details, one hand already fiddling under the cassock. But there was no absolution for these women: at the end of it was just a sticky mess to be wiped up with a tissue.

The funny thing was, most of these 'confessions' were sent in by men: they invented the sin and then confessed it. What vivid imaginations! Anyone would think it was they who wanted to be stripped, dominated, fucked, ejaculated into. Was there a hidden yearning in these men to be feminine? Temporarily, of course. Not to lend a hand with the ironing, but to know how good their fucking felt from the inside. These correspondents claimed all kinds of pleasure-giving powers, but since they could never feel the ecstasy they hoped they were providing they had to hear some sign, to have each thrust matched by a submissive whimper and grunted profanity. That's why they got so narked when women just lay there.

One or two of the letters looked genuine enough (you could tell by the handwriting and the little details a man would have missed). But as often as not I had to make them up myself.

My experience of being fucked was obviously limited, but I was determined to sound authentic. In a quest for accuracy I asked female friends all kinds of intimate questions. Some tried to help, but were hopelessly vague.

'Well, it's just sort of nice, it's like sort of warm and floaty.'

But 'just sort of nice' wasn't what *Fiesta* readers paid their money for. They wanted women who gasped at the size of their pricks, groaned with pleasure, talked dirty, begged for more. Each reader imagined himself as the man these women were talking about. A verdict of 'just sort of nice' would have made them hang their heads in shame.

Some verged on the sarcastic: 'Let me stick this broom handle up your arse and see how you like it.' Quite uncalled for, really. Others told me to imagine Tone fondling my arse and sticking his cheese and onion flavoured tongue down my throat. How romantic would I feel?

Still, I had a job to do. Three confessions every issue. Before long, for a couple of hours a month, I had to be a part-time woman. I was the 'I' who unbuckled her bra and admired her breasts in the bedroom mirror; I was the 'I' who wishfully fingered her fanny while having a bath. I also had to be the 'I' who fancied the plumber, slipped my hand inside his overalls to cup his balls, slide my fingers around his throbbing hard-on. Simple verbs weren't enough for the readers, it was the adjectives and the subjectivity that mattered, the bone-hardness of his erection, the taste of his knob, the warm wetness of my fanny, the hoarseness of my appreciative cries.

How easy it was to play the part. I prided myself on my ventriloqual skills. I could change at will, I could be a slim student in T-shirt and jeans, a factory girl with a dirty mind, a bored housewife waiting for the milkman to call, a middle-aged matron gasping for the attentions of a horny youth. As a youngster I'd sat waiting for Calliope and Clio to give me ideas, now I was sitting here staring into space and my muses were women from a bus queue.

Was it authentic? No one ever complained. And that worried me: if it sounded so authentic, did it mean I had homosexual leanings? I was genuinely worried. What if it crept up on me unnoticed, became a way of thinking, so that one day I'd have to quietly leave the country and get a job in a Bangkok TV bar, a sad middle-aged man who was neither one sex nor another, living in a twilight world of drugs and prostitution.

If Janice had a number-one bugbear, aside from the pervy phone calls, it had to be the postman. He always had a grin for her, doubly wide on the occasions when he handed a thick package through the glass hatchway.

'More of them Readers' Wives, I bet,' he ventured, one morning. Keeping secrets from a vigilant postman is impossible. 'Scandalous what blokes get up to soon as they've got one of them Polaroids.'

Janice snatched the package and flung it into the In Tray.

'I don't comment on things like that.'

'Wouldn't get my wife doing it.'

Janice made her boredom patently clear by retiring behind a copy of _19_. But the postman was in no hurry, he didn't mind talking to a brick wall.

'Won't even have her picture taken in a bikini down at Clacton. Thinks she's fat. She ain't! Ain't slim, no, I wouldn't say that; but she ain't fat neither. Nothing that couldn't be put right if she'd lay off them Jaffa Cakes day in day out.'

Janice shoved her nose deeper into the magazine, no doubt looking for advice about postmen who always positioned themselves so that they could peer into her blouse.

'Course, you ain't got that problem, Janice.'

'What problem's that?'

'Fat. There's no fat on you. You're just the right weight for your height. Your statistics are in proportion. The lads wouldn't complain seeing you in Readers' Wives. You ought to get your boyfriend to—'

'Why don't you fuck off and get on with your job?' suggested Janice.

'Just making conversation.'

The postie grabbed his sack and scuttled out through the door. They never did speak much to each other after that. Whenever she had to sign for a Recorded Delivery, Janice shunned his official Royal Mail pen and used her own, as if fearful of catching something from the chewed-up end.

The opposite to Readers' Wives was Celebrity Skin. Magazines got hold of all kinds of peeping-Tom shots: film stars getting out of cars with no knickers on; lounging topless by the poolside. Glimpses of celebrity nipple took on the significance of holy relics. The pictures were grainy, the stray nipples no more remarkable than any other woman's nipple, but it was who they belonged to that mattered.

It was surprising how many household names had secrets. They'd all been hard-up and taken part in films they regretted. Even in Britain we had our secrets: like bespectacled Olive from *On the Buses*, who'd done some nude modelling; and sweet Sally Geeson, the teenage daughter from *Bless This House*, showing her boobs in a sexy film called *Sauce for the Goose*, with Norman Wisdom.

Stars have the same anatomy as wives and girlfriends – even the iconic Marilyn Monroe, in the nude, was no more or less wonderful than the woman next door. Celebrity nudity, paradoxically, is not an ultimate prize but rather an antithesis: it gives the lie to all the hype.

In the USA, *Playboy* and *Penthouse* still offer tens of thousands of dollars to film and TV stars to show the lot. Not only celebrities, but any woman who hits the headlines for whatever reason.

Fiesta got into this in a modest way by employing Rosie Swale, the famous yachtswoman. Dennis had seen some photos of her on the deck of a yacht in the tabloids and thought it would be a great sales boost. And for sure, *Fiesta*'s readers loved it. This woman was a spunky adventurer, a skinny blonde with a lot to say for herself.

* * *

I'm writing to ask if you need any sexy men to photograph for your magazine. My 8" prick is admired by many people, especially the women who have been privileged to feel its electrifying sexual effects. I pose nude at the local art college part-time and am in popular demand with the lady students. I can add a degree of horny realism to any photo session. Your models will appreciate working with a professional guy who can bring some authentic moistening to their sex areas . . .

CVs from would-be studs landed on our desks with monotonous regularity. They were convinced that Galaxy's magazines were just a front: behind it was a secret THRUSH-like organization, busy making porno movies, arranging orgies, supplying hunks to service rich women. Hush-hush of course, but those in the know knew we were always in search of fresh talent.

Sometimes they sent a mugshot: men with intense eyes shot against the crumpled orange curtains of a photo booth. It wasn't that they looked weird, not really, not physically

– apart from the home-visit haircut. What usually caused a ripple of unease was the expression: a thin-lipped beam of self-assurance, an unblinking reaction to the flash.

Others wanted their equipment to speak for itself – hence the muddy Polaroid prick-shot, a plum-headed erection poking proudly out from below a grubby polo shirt, snapped via the dressing-table mirror.

Obsessed by porno fame and a vision of limitless free fucks, these selfless volunteers were more than happy to waive the fee. Just as well. Getting mixed up with such nutters would have been fatal. Sometimes, spitefully, we speared their stupid faces to our memo boards with drawing pins. Or, if they looked too much like axe murderers, crazed by loneliness, we flicked their greasy snapshots into the bin, anxious to be rid of them for good.

Galaxy had no need of outside help – why should they when it was all too easy to press-gang its own employees into helping out as extras when needed . . .

For late commuters on the 9.56 Croydon–Victoria it was destined to be a day they'd remember. Men who peeped from behind their newspapers at secretarial legs were in for a real treat. They were about to see the *Fiesta* Flasher, one of our hit features. Models would be dispatched to expose their tits and suspenders in well-known spots – Windsor Castle, Stonehenge, Portsmouth Docks. Most sessions, timidly, took place at dawn when the risk of being copped was minimal. Never mind, *Fiesta*'s readers loved to think that they were in on it, part of the dispatching of naked stormtroopers into the heart of prim middle-class Britain. That's just what they needed, all those old biddies, retired majors, penny-pinching shopkeepers: a close-up of knickers and nipples! It was flashing by proxy. All the scandal (and the photos to prove it), but none of the risk.

Always desperate for new ideas, Dennis hit on this one when he caught me browsing through a book called *The Age Of Steam*. A flasher on a railway station. Not just any old station, mind – Clapham Junction, a railway record-beater, the busiest station in the world. And guess who'd go along to play the part of the scandalized trainspotter . . .

Notebook and biro in hand, I stood in an open-mouthed pose. As the trains rattled by to Surbiton and Croydon, Lucy whipped open her fur coat. You could just catch a ten-second pantomime inside the carriages: newspapers snapped down and goggle eyes appeared at the windows, noses pressed against nicotined glass for a last desperate glimpse of this free striptease. The driver of a shunting engine leaned from his cab, mesmerized. One false move and he'd have catapulted his empty wagon halfway down to Wandsworth.

'Oi!'

We'd been spotted. Railway workers, like policemen, have an unerring nose for funny business. Commuters without tickets, jaywalking trainspotters, passengers without knickers, they'll nab 'em. From the far side of the station, half a dozen platforms away, some railway bod was yelling at us, but his complaint was whipped away by the roar of a passing Gatwick Express. We carried on snapping. A minute later a red-cheeked lad appeared at the top of the stairs and came nervously towards us. He looked terrified.

'The station master's sent me over. He wants to know what you're doing.'

'Press,' I said, flashing my NUJ card at him. I'd only recently got it and flashed it at every opportunity. 'Just taking a few pictures.'

'You can't take photographs on railway property,' he insisted, making sideways glances at Lucy's breasts peaking out of the flasher's coat. Oddly enough he made no mention of the nudity. Perhaps it wasn't against railway by-laws. 'You need permission from divisional headquarters.'

'Two more, Lucy.'

The photographer backed away from her, adjusting his dials. Lucy forced her chattering teeth into a smile and let her coat fall open. The youth gaped. If he hadn't been under orders he'd have loved every second of it.

'You can get permission . . .' he mumbled. 'If you write to the divisional manager at Waterloo.'

'S'alright.' Phil was already packing his cameras. 'We've got it wrapped up now.'

Lucy turned to the youth and stood with her hands in her pockets, flapping open the coat to give him a full-frontal view. Protected by me and the photographer she could find it a hilarious tease. The youth's eyes popped like balls hitting a pinball score. Lucy giggled cruelly. Then she wrapped up and lit a Dunhill.

The episode had an unexpected twist.

During the Falklands war Russell Gay sent out thousands of mags to 'our boys'. Oddly, such gestures are an accepted part of the war effort, real patriotism, and good publicity for the publisher. Quite what officers think about their lads wanking themselves silly on the eve of battle, no one knows. Funnily enough, no one seems to mind in these circumstances: in war men are fighters and deserve as many fucks as they can get as a reward.

Eight thousand miles away a friend from school who I hadn't seen for ten years was relaxing after a day's duty in the Falklands Task Force. Flicking through some of the mags he came to the *Fiesta* Flasher and did a double-take.

'I know him!' He showed the mag to his mates. 'I went to school with him.'

Since they are so full of pussy, maybe it's no surprise that girlie mags have nine lives. Or more. Some seem virtually indestructible. Hoarded in secret piles for years or thrown out in bin bags which split and spill their shameful contents in the street, they turn up in the unlikeliest places at the most awkward times. Only recently I was sitting outside the local library, reading, when my eye was drawn to the litter bin. Though not normally given to rummaging in bins, I couldn't help noticing half a dozen magazines. Shoving my hand into this tramp's bran tub I retrieved half a dozen *Mayfairs* from the mid-seventies. My first reaction was to hang on to them, but a sense of shame, of being seen, made me return them. No doubt the council bin operative kept them for himself. (And why is it that when pages of the *Sun* drift down a desolate street, it's always Page Three that lands at your feet?)

I don't like to think how many copies of that *Fiesta* are still in circulation. Thousands, I guess. What a thought ... that beardless young man still lives, hidden away in some bloke's cache of porn mags. But I'm not unique. Madonna may get away with her youthful antics as a pin-up; but how many less fortunate women, now wives and mothers, live in dread of having a secret past revealed, of being drummed out of the local Rotary Club or the PTA? In the unlikely event that I ever get famous that picture may yet come back to haunt me. The tabloids would love it: 'Booker prizewinner's secret porno life!'

In addition to the six regular pages of Readers' Wives, Dennis invited the most popular ones along to our studios for the star treatment – specially designed sets, proper lighting and direction, professional photography. And a fee. But these occasions were not without drama.

So much for Janice's dedication to security. When it came to it she let any old nutter wander in. This one was brandishing a breadknife – and he didn't look like he'd come in to help with the sandwiches. He waved the blade wildly and sliced a sheet of paper out of Colin's typewriter.

'Come on, where is she?'

'Who?'

'Ma wife. I know you've got her here, stripping off for your pervert readers.'

Obviously not a man in tune with the new thinking on wifely nudity. But, hang on, hadn't she arrived with her husband? Who was that guy in the studio with her? A lover, it seemed. One who'd not only been screwing the wife in question, but was brazen enough to send photographic evidence to a girlie mag! He was in big trouble.

Rumours of aggro had already reached the studio. Our model's short 'n' curlies straightened with terror at the news that her husband was in the building. Getting wind of a bruising-to-come the stand-in husband put down his complimentary Twiglet, drained his wine glass and made for the fire exit. Just in time. The doors rattled under a rain of kicks, then flew open as the cuckold made a grand entrance with his breadknife.

'You fucking slag!' he yelled. 'Why, why, why?'

He crashed to the floor in a sobbing heap, narrowly avoiding hara-kiri. His wife covered herself with a robe and knelt beside him, kissing his forehead and promising to come back to him. No, that nasty man wouldn't persuade her to do naughty pictures again. Geoff picked up the breadknife and put it safely on a shelf: it would make a useful little saw if it wasn't reclaimed.

The next studio session was less traumatic. The couple were well-spoken and charming. Their breeding was obvious as they ignored the cheese and onion crisps and homed in on the smoked salmon and the shrimp vol-au-vents. To partake of dainty comestibles in the buff requires a whole new etiquette. Does one brush the crumbs of flaky pastry from one's pubes? Is it proper to use a cheese straw to remove fluff from the navel? Would a serviette only make one's nudity a topic for vulgar comments?

The fella amiably agreed to pose for 'One for the Ladies', a male pin-up we put in to please our female readers.

After saying goodbye to them, we thought no more of it until the pictures were published a few months later. In a *News of the World* our two naked stars were front-page news. They'd been run out of town! It turned out the lady was a primary-school teacher, her boyfriend a lay preacher (who obviously did more laying than preaching!) and the decent folks in their village were not having those kind of people in contact with their children.

We were baffled. Why, when they were so certain to be found out, had they been so keen to do it? No one was forcing them. Perhaps they were so bored with village life they decided to go out in a blaze of glory and damn the Mrs Grundys and Henry Hypocrites.

'Fat bastard!'

Rich, the post boy, glared out of the pub window as Russell settled his plumpness into the driving seat of his Mercedes.

'Where's he off to now – some fancy fucking lunch at the Savoy?'

'Fancy' wasn't a word that could be applied to our lunch – two pints of lager, ham roll for Rich, crisps for me. Rich yanked his payslip from his pocket and waved it in my face.

'I'm on a fucking pittance while he's driving about in a fancy limo.'

Rich may have been glorified as 'Mail & Communications Supervisor', but to us he was the post boy. He licked labels, lugged parcels, sent off back issues, and did anything else Russell told him to.

The company's subscription service was a boon to lily-livered men. Instead of risking embarrassment at their local newsagent's, they had their *Knave*s and *Fiesta*s delivered in a plain brown envelope. But even plain brown envelopes attract suspicion. Men who mistrusted their wives had the mag sent to their business address instead.

Rich had a master plan to get rich. His job gave him ready access to Galaxy's mailing list and in his quiet moments he'd been browsing through it.

'There's all sorts on it,' he told me. 'MPs. Look, care of the House of Commons. Entrepreneurs. I read about this one in the paper – he owns a chain of freezer shops. Guys with money.' He paused. 'Guys who don't want their wives to know the kind of things they read . . .'

He gave me a smile. The same kind of smile Ronnie Biggs probably had when he said: 'There's this train, see.'

His brain had been fucked up by the chemicals in the

address labels, that was my guess. Self-adhesive ones were too expensive for Galaxy. Why squander money when you had an employee with a tongue? In between the rhythmic chugging of the franking machine I could hear him muttering, one minute totting up the figures needed for a Gibson Les Paul, then reproducing the sound of one, screeching out 'Layla' in a tooth-grinding falsetto.

'There's a fatal flaw in your plan,' I pointed out a few days later. No one else seemed bothered, but Rich could land himself in deep trouble if someone didn't intervene. 'What if they'd rather pay some heavies to sort you out?'

My suggestion made him pale. Rich had a fertile imagination. In less than a day he'd decided that his plan wasn't so clever, after all.

Elaine had no objections to my work. Flicking through the occasional *Fiesta* I brought home, she had a good snigger over the letters, the jokes and the dodgy snapshots. I worried about what she might think, but she didn't appear to be threatened by it or insulted. I often tried to imagine what my feelings might be, if the roles were reversed and Elaine were coming home and showing me photographs of naked men in suggestive postures. I couldn't.

Feminist-minded friends urged me to give it up before it was too late. For what reason they wouldn't specify, apart from hinting darkly about some catastrophic moral meltdown. But why should I give up a well-paid job in order to satisfy someone else's moral smugness? Would I ask them to give up theirs? Since they were friends, I happily told them to get lost.

I had to be more wary with women who didn't know me as well. I'd learned to be discreet. If anyone asked, I just said I worked in journalism. But some people in the pub thought it great fun to drop me in it.

'He works for one of them mucky books, love.'

I was more ashamed about having lied. My fibbing merely let them know my weakness. And yes, I always assumed people, women, would think the worst, look at me and walk away in disgust. It happened now and then, but I usually shrugged it off. My biggest dread was to be slagged off loudly in the middle of the pub and have a pint of beer poured over my head.

I didn't mind a good-humoured argument – there were issues worth discussing. But I wasn't always on the defensive. Sometimes I flared up: did these women think they had a copyright on feminism? Some of them were only fellow-travellers, anxious to be on the bandwagon, eager to avenge all the various slights, jiltings and non-arriving orgasms they'd suffered. As an illegitimate child I had felt the consequences of male deceit and treachery as keenly as any of them had. Maybe more so. Any guilt I felt about my job, well, I would deal with that in my own way, not tolerate a lecture from them.

The only person I'd have tolerated a lecture from was my mum. She had no idea what I'd got myself into, and I didn't want her to find out. If she had, and protested, I'd have felt honour bound to listen.

But even in sophisticated London, feminists were far from being a majority. Most women, though mildly scandalized by my CV, were only too eager to find out all the details. Nosiness always won out over any hazy stance on decency and political correctness.

Any indignation usually stemmed from a gross misunderstanding about the function of girlie mags. Teenagers satisfying their curiosity, they could understand that. They even felt charitably inclined towards loners, no-hopers and middle-aged men in loveless marriages. But such stereotypes only misled. They knew a dozen ways in which their fella didn't match those photofits. Mr X was a sexist bore, while their fella was witty and charming and enlightened; Mrs X was a shrewish spoilsport, while they'd spent a fortune on Janet Reger knickers and couldn't wait for the next lovemaking session.

So no way would their man need a dirty mag. Why would

any man who was getting his ration? After adultery and VD, partners with a secret porn habit are every woman's nightmare. Jealousy, guilt, anger, betrayal, disappointment – the reactions are various, but something's certainly wrong with the relationship!

Many of these women have a fixed idea that sexual intercourse is a zenith, wanking, a sad and lonesome nadir. The two activities are worlds apart: success and failure, riches and poverty, beauty and ugliness. Sex is fireworks on a crisp winter's night, girlie mags a dead match in a bucket.

But maybe it wasn't the pictures that the women objected to. More disturbing were all the clues about the way men thought, the way they acted behind women's backs, their secret sexuality. Women have been led to believe that all men want to do is lay them, come and clear off to the pub. This lack of romance annoys the hell out of them, but at least they know where they stand. What shocked a lot of the women I talked to were things like the readers' letters. It unnerved them to think of men sitting down and filling sheet after sheet with filth and spunky fantasies. And what about men dressing up in stockings, being turned on by shoes, fantasizing over fatties and tarts and women prisoners? What the hell did it all mean? They wanted their fellas to be predictable, controllable, pathetic.

For some men, the moral support they get from girlie mags is just as important as the pin-ups. Under siege from a world full of feminists and cocky women, they can retreat into a comforting fictional world. A real matey scene; the talk is crude and the jokes are dirty. No need to mind your language. A prick's a prick and a fuck's a fuck, none of that fancy talk about making love. Hell, a man can't be doing with concepts like affection when he's got a hard-on to deal with.

But on another level men need the mags because women don't understand them. A healthy sex life sounds great, but that is only a euphemism for officially approved. Male sexuality isn't the simple thrust and come process some women think it is. Rather, it's a complex rag-bag of fetishes and desires. The problem is that a uniform set of urges is proscribed by the combined forces of peer pressure, shyness and women's expectations. Men want to express themselves, do their own thing. They want to talk about it, but generally no one wants to listen. A man might want his girlfriend to pose in red high-heels and black suspenders while he sits back and masturbates, but few women will indulge him. So rather than risk ridicule and rows, men just go off and buy a mag instead. It makes life a lot simpler.

Men are always boasting of their weapons. If the truth is known they often get frightened. Pricks have a life of their own, jerking up and down like signals on a busy branch line. Testicles hum with pre-programmed zeal, leading men into situations that every logical fibre warns them against. Is it any wonder that, bravado aside, they sometimes fear losing control?:

> I have just measured the circumference of my
> testicles and discovered that one is 0.5 mm
> smaller than the other. Does this mean I am
> susceptible to cancer? My uncle had to have a
> wooden leg due to this . . .

Fiesta had its own 'Dear Doctor' to help alleviate correspondents' doubts and fears. He was ex-public school, down on his luck and grateful for the monthly fee. But sympathy wasn't his strong suit, especially when it came to sorting out the tangled sex lives of the working classes:

> I recently asked my neighbour if he would
> mind inseminating my wife for me, as I have
> been sterile for the past ten years and we're
> desperate for another child before it's too late.
> He's a good sort and always willing to do a
> favour. I was prepared to give them half-a-

dozen sessions, but my suspicions were
aroused when the meetings went on for over a
month and, against my wishes, included oral
sex, which I argued had no place in the concep-
tion process. Now they want me to pack my
bags and go. What do you advise?

To the doctor, brought up on the Classics, a council-estate
housewife on heat would have been as terrifying as a Mino-
taur. 'This is, to some extent, a scenario of your own
making,' he responded, frankly but unhelpfully.

For some reason *Fiesta* had been adopted by men with trans-
vestite leanings. Most of them claimed to be powerfully
hetero – they just wanted to share the pleasures of silk and
satin next to their skin. Along with their letters, they sent
in Polaroids taken via the bedroom mirror. Wispy black
panties stretched across muscular thighs, wiry pubes
sprouting above the waistband. They squeezed their booze-
fed tits into Wonderbras, slipped on creamy blouses and
posed with them cheekily unbuttoned. How could they
equate this with femininity? While their mates spent the
weekends up a ladder slapping emulsion on the garage
wall, these transvestites hid behind closed curtains lovingly
painting their nails with tiny brushes, razoring their legs
and rolling on pantihose.
    We had a good laugh at these snaps, but I couldn't help
a twinge of guilt. They were right in some ways, these
mutant lorry drivers and factory workers; femininity was
denied, men were still squeezed into stifling roles. I
admired their single-mindedness, but I feared for their
recklessness:

During a visit to the in-laws I made an excuse
and went upstairs to the bathroom. They
thought I'd gone for a piss, but I had other
reasons! My mother-in-law, a shapely lady of

52, keeps her Ali Baba laundry basket in there and I quickly rummaged through to find some of her underwear – settling on one of her 36B brassières and a pair of knickers which had a tasteful cornflower pattern around the waistband. Slipping out of my clothes and into these garments, I was soon enjoying a delicious wank.

All of a sudden my world caved in! In the middle of my masturbating I'd had a stroke and the next thing I knew about it I was in intensive care. The doctor has told me I'm lucky to be alive and will need my family's love and care when I come out. But my wife is now suing for divorce and my own family has disowned me. What on earth am I to do? Is this the price I must pay for trying to get five minutes' pleasure in this godforsaken world? Please help me. I am at my wits' end!

They could never be what they yearned to be: burly and unshaven bodies just didn't fit into smooth and silky clothes. The stresses of a split-sex personality were hard to imagine. Perhaps *Fiesta*'s noblest function here was not as a wank mag, but as a confessional.

Now and then I bumped into an unlikely saint, a man who claimed that he'd never heard of *Fiesta* or *Penthouse*, let alone looked at one. I didn't believe them. Smug and smiling in their polo-neck sweaters and Hush Puppies, these men were so desperate to be 'new men' that they'd totally lost touch with their balls. A more boring bunch you couldn't expect to meet outside a monastery. And the thing was, women didn't seem to like them very much either. They radiated a kind of sexless anti-charm. Women seemed even more wary of this bunch than they were of men who read girlie mags.

Or was it me who was wrong? Did I really believe that all men were kinky, sex-mad? Had I, without noticing, slipped into an amoral state of mind? The year before Elaine, I'd been out with at least eight girls. It wasn't as though I'd ever thought of myself as handsome or even charming. Quite the opposite. It was a source of wonder to me that I ever managed to get off with anyone. It just happened.

But had these facts ever been offered as evidence in some hypothetical court case I'd have been condemned. 'M'lud, we are looking at a man with an insatiable appetite for casual sex, a man to whom relationships mean nothing. The evidence speaks for itself.' The jury would ponder the evidence, but they'd be divided. Then the clincher: 'He also has a full-time job on a pornographic magazine, which is full of naked females and text of a depraved nature . . .'

So I'd have been exactly the same person if I'd landed a job at *Goldfish Monthly*. It was no use blaming my work. I felt ashamed in the presence of the saints. What if there was an awful synchronicity about it all, what if *Fiesta* was my natural habitat? Maybe being at *Fiesta* was what I deserved. I'd quickly picked up the basics of journalism, so if I'd been at *Goldfish Monthly* I'd have probably pissed off long ago. But I found sex endlessly fascinating. Why deny it? Anyone who claimed indifference was a liar. I was often surprised at what the post brought, but very rarely offended. I spent half my working day sniggering at men's vanity and insecurities. Occasionally the typing and the clerical stuff got boring, but at the end of the day it wasn't naked women, readers' letters or the bureaucratic tedium that bugged me, just the two-faced attitudes of other people. A rebellious streak made me carry on, just to spite them.

5 Kilburn Narratives

The mechanics stood by, smoking and grinning, as Rich puffed up and down Galaxy's stairs with his rocking piles of cardboard boxes. Now and then a loud cheer erupted, like when they caught a glimpse of a knobbly black dildo, or when an inflatable woman winked at them through the cellophane window of her box.

'Keep them shittin' boxes shut!' snapped Janice as he staggered through reception. 'What kind of sickos need that stuff anyway?' she demanded of anyone who'd stop and listen.

She and her boyfriend obviously didn't. Anyone who wanted to check on Janice's sexual sobriety was always welcome to inspect the engagement ring. In a few months they'd be married. The wedding-present list had been circulated. It had everything a modern couple could possibly need: wine glasses, towels, sandwich toaster, pine spice rack. No mention of a multi-speed vibrator (requires four AA 1.5v batteries) or a vacuum developer. Janice was all for the 'his and hers' concept, but not when it came to marital aids.

'What do they get married for in the first place if they need that kind of gear?'

Russell, always on for a business opportunity, had leased out a room to a company called Cupid Products. Marital aids was a multi-million pound industry and he fancied a share of it. The gear may not have been on wedding lists, but someone out there was buying it by the boxload.

Years before Louise and Kim became famous actresses they were poor drama students. Not long after I went across the road, they moved into the flat next door to Guy, turning it into yet another epicentre of girlishness.

Louise had a gooseberry, a thirtysomething widow who'd been in the local am-dram society with her. Every other weekend she came down on the train from Leicester and tagged along to share the buzz. They tried to be polite, but Linda's starstruck enthusiasm embarrassed them. On one occasion she rang to say she was on her way, but Louise and Kim were otherwise engaged.

So it was that I found the cheerful Linda sitting on their doorstep one Saturday. Did I know where Louise was? Yes, I did, but I wasn't going to pass that information on.

I shrugged. Embarrassed silence. A fatal silence. So why did I think it was my job to fill it? She looked so crestfallen I said the first thing that came into my head: come in for a cuppa. I still had my key to the old flat and Guy didn't mind me letting myself in. If Guy had been at home, if I'd simply gone back to Elaine and spent the afternoon shopping, none of the rest would have happened.

Perked up by the tea, Linda told me about her dreams. So what if she was thirtysomething – that wouldn't stop her getting into drama school.

'It's burning inside me, Nick.'

'What is?'

'Ambition.'

A break, that's all she needed. She'd spent a fortune on publicity photographs and fancy CVs. The paper was impressive, dimpled and ivory-tinted, but the contents were hardly riveting: housewife, part-time secretary, dinner lady and, in between, moments of small-town fame, Goneril and the woman with the headache in *Abigail's Party*. If only one of the RADA scouts would come up to Leicester and see her. She'd even send them the train fare.

Since I was there, would I help her rehearse her lines for *Much Ado About Nothing*? We sat on the bed, but only because there was nowhere else to sit. What was it – the smell of sheets, the squeak of springs, the way the suspension just naturally threw people towards one another? Whatever, it seemed to exert a mischievous aura of its own. Maybe. Or maybe that's rubbish. Blaming the furniture is a laughable excuse.

How difficult acting must be, I mused. The things you had to do off the cuff: scream, cry, take off your clothes. I knew how desperately she wanted to prove herself. What about having to kiss, how did you make it look real?

She rose to the challenge, pushing me back on the bed, ruffling my hair, sticking her excited tongue between my lips, streaking the inside of my cheeks with the peppery tang of Aquafresh. Was that real enough?

Too real. I'd only been flirting, just to reassure myself I still had the pull. I enjoyed the domesticated life with Elaine, but I missed the crazy old days too.

Guy came back five minutes later, or things would have gone too far.

Louise was aghast when I told her what I'd done. But even in her first year at college she'd been tipped for stardom, so I dismissed her Cassandra act as histrionics.

The following Tuesday Elaine and I were woken by the postman. I padded downstairs, zipping my flies. He wanted me to sign for a Recorded Delivery. The postmark was Leicester. I pocketed the letter before Elaine saw it and rushed off to work. I had an awful premonition that Louise's concern might be right:

Dearest Nick,
Saturday was the most exciting thing that has
happened to me since my husband died. You
are a kind and considerate friend (I refer to
your help with the reading). You have started a
fire within me.

It was the time of the month when I knocked together the readers' letters, sorted through the jotted and scrolled insanities of the sex-obsessed. But that day the most alarming letter was in my pocket. And there was no escape, it was addressed to me personally.

Two days later, the postman rang the bell with another Recorded Delivery. Then the phone calls started.

'There's a Mrs something on the phone,' yelled Janice, calling me away from the coffee machine.

I didn't have the sense to be embarrassed. I loved the filthy looks Janice gave me, revelled in the rumours she quickly spread about me seeing a married woman. I didn't have a clue. I'd started a fire all right. I'd become a crucial part of Linda's strategy. Having a base in Belsize Park would be perfect. All she had to do was become my lover and move in. She'd be close to Louise, handy for doing the rounds of drama schools, to make those quality contacts only London could offer. She'd be able to get *The Stage* hot off the press instead of having to wait two days for it to arrive at her local paper shop.

Crank phone calls were an occupational hazard at Galaxy. Janice guillotined most of them with the fuck-off cut-off, but sometimes they fooled her with plausible stories about researching an article from a past issue. So she put them through to Editorial. Halfway through what sounded like a polite enquiry (and you could always sense the change in key) they'd switch to Nuremberg-rally mode, bawling us out from their telephonic pulpits:

'You think you're so clever, you people. Corrupting decent women. Selling pictures of them when you've had your way. The Lord will summon you to be judged, you evil scum.'

Sometimes she put them through just for a laugh. She had to deal with them all day – how did we like it?

I didn't mind a laugh. Or even a row. What I hated was the familiarity. The kind of magazine *Fiesta* was excused them the usual protocol. You'd pick up the phone and there'd be this nasal Midlander who took you for a kindred spirit, a saloon-bar dosser with a foam-dampened moustache and an arsenal of dirty jokes.

'Do you want to see my wife's fanny? Tight as a gorilla's handshake, know what I mean? She wants to come along and have her photograph taken for them Readers' Wives.'

I developed an intuitive skill for detecting bad breath, just by the way it crackled in the earpiece. I even imagined I could tell the precise foulness of it – onions, wet dog, sour milk, those cheesey biscuit snacks sold in pubs. Why was it so impossible to imagine anyone with healthy teeth and gleaming gums betraying secrets about his wife?

'Piss off' would have been the obvious response. But we weren't allowed to say that. These were our readers (allegedly) so we had a duty to be patient and professional. Even if they were having a go at us, Dennis wanted us to write down their comments. Consumer feedback was a valuable indicator of whether we were doing our job properly.

So this was our jury, this faceless brotherhood of wankers and sleazeballs?

The Internet hadn't yet been invented. Ceefax offered no on-screen pages for perverts. We were the obvious source of secret info. Where could you get videos of women wrestling in jelly? Was it possible to meet models on a Platonic basis? Could we get them some prints of that set with the naked blonde on the back seat of a Bentley? What issue was that? Oh, you know, it was 1978 or 1979. Maybe 1980. Definitely 1981 at the latest.

Boring stuff. But, at the end of the day, *Fiesta* was only a kind of hobby magazine, a lifestyle bible – and readers relied on us for our expertise and our advice.

Some were harmless enough, though. From the USA we had the Tennessee Tosser. At 10 a.m. Kilburn time he was just getting home. Totally zonked by his night at the local bar, his sodden voice crackled across the world via satellite. His guitar strings had bust, he'd lost a chance of a recording contract in Nashville, his woman had packed her bags. The transatlantic phone link and an inch of bourbon was all he had to keep him sane. Why he picked on us I couldn't figure. He never even mentioned the magazine. Maybe *Fiesta*'s number was confusingly similar to the Chattanooga Samaritans and he'd accidentally added the international code for London. Sometimes, in a better mood, he'd be chewing pizza and, with his new set of strings on, he'd strum a few chords and ask us what we thought of his chances of hitting the big time.

Why was I jeopardizing everything by this dangerous liaison with Linda? Even Guy was concerned: 'Nick, she's obviously desperate.'

I resented the slur, as if I could only attract the lonely and the desperate.

Guy had never wholly forgiven Elaine for breaking up our bachelor lifestyle. But at least she was pretty and domesticated and intelligent. Why was I risking it all for a fuck?

It wasn't just a fuck, that was the problem. I'd been with Elaine for two years and we both took each other for granted. Linda's flattery turned my head. According to Linda I was sexy, cool-headed and intelligent. Though she hardly knew me, I fell for it. I was desperate to believe. I still remembered the kiss. The danger. That's what I'd missed. Not sex, but that first kiss. Couples had sex, but it was routine. They quickly forgot to kiss each other, or if they did it was a ritual peck, as exciting as a handshake. You never recaptured that heart-thumping first time.

Guy was right, though. I had a cosy set-up with Elaine. We got along fine. She cooked for me, talked with me, slept with me. A man shouldn't want anything more. Affairs were risky enough at the best of times, but if I got myself ensnarled with Linda it wouldn't just be a sneaky screw once a week, it'd be a serious takeover bid. Linda would want me to ditch Elaine, boot her out so that she could move in.

She knew about Elaine, of course, but insisted I deserved better. And she'd show me how much.

'You're a man, Nick. You need a proper woman, someone who understands your needs. Not some silly kid. Get rid of her.'

Linda rang and invited me for a weekend in Leicester – two whole days together, she promised. I'd made up my mind to cool it off, but being wanted weakened my resolve.

She met me at the station and man-handled me into a waiting taxi. She was proud of me – she wanted the taxi driver to know about her catch. She fumbled with me behind his back, but I felt like the male equivalent of a blow-up doll.

Back at her neat semi she relaxed me with a drink, unzipped me amd got to work. But bonking was only part of it. For Linda, the weekend wasn't just sex, it was her chance to show off her good points – the neat housekeeping, the home cooking. Linda's eagerness exhausted me. Not just the hungry performance on the sofa and in the bed, but the way she rushed to pour my beer, light my cigarette. I just wanted a mistress, but she wanted more – another husband, a friend, a protector. How could I make those promises to her?

The next day, after tea in bed and early-morning sex, the guilt hit me. Big double-decker guilt with all the trimmings. Infidelity was bad enough; lying naked in another woman's bed on a Saturday morning. But this Saturday of all Saturdays – Elaine's birthday!

I couldn't get away fast enough. Linda tried to hide her disappointment. What about Sunday lunch? She'd bought the best joint in the butcher's, selected the new potatoes one by one to get the sweetest, even bought a bottle of wine.

She didn't have to say it, I said it to myself. You fucking bastard. You awful fucking bastard. I hated myself for what I'd done. For betraying Elaine most of all, but for spoiling Linda's plans too.

She insisted on seeing me off. Dolled up in pink hot pants she walked arm in arm with me through the streets of Leicester. I thought everyone was staring at us. The benchful of youths, the smirking bus driver, all those shoppers – they all knew. Maybe they were just looking at Linda's legs. No, they could see straight through us. Who did they despise most, the desperate widow or the exploiting chancer? Their stares said: he doesn't mind fucking her, but he's ashamed to walk down the street with her.

It was nearly teatime when I got back to London. The bedsit was empty. I grabbed a taxi for Paddington, got a train to Henley-on-Thames, and arrived at Elaine's house panting. I hadn't even got her a card. I tried to laugh it off, drag her out for a drink. But I knew she'd registered something was going on. My burbling lies about visiting an old friend would never make it better.

Overseeing the whole marital-aids operation was Trevor, the pot-bellied Cockney in charge of Cupid Products. If I'd talked to Trevor about my domestic problems he'd have recommended something from his range of products. He was proud of the services he offered. Cupid, according to their adverts, could provide the modern couple with everything they needed to explore their sexuality within a loving relationship.

'It's all down to lack of variety,' was his universal diagnosis.

To revive a marriage, all a wife needed to do was wear a frilly négligé and a pair of crotchless panties. All her guy had to do was snap on a coloured condom and give it squirt of Stud 100 Delay Spray. According to Trevor, marital aids should have been recognized as one of the great boons of twentieth-century life. Bona fide medical treatment. Instead of coming out with a load of waffle and bullshit, marriage-guidance wallahs should have prescription pads like doctors. They should be trained to identify the real roots of marriage problems: if a man wasn't satisfying a woman they should suggest a genital examination. Maybe he just wasn't big enough, so they could offer vacuum development treatment. Women would be encouraged to 'explore their own sexuality'. Companies like Cupid would clean up by wholesaling dildoes to the NHS.

Some people still thought of Cupid as a curly mopped cherub with a bow and arrow. Twee, sickly, old hat. Cupid, like Elvis or Madonna, wasn't just a person, he was a small industry, incorporated and with limited liability. He was a hard-headed business chap who dealt not in pink and satin abstracts, but in the hardware of love. Love wasn't a spontaneous thing any more, not in this modern world: you needed all the gadgets to go with it. Somewhere out there, in Leeds or Taiwan, was a factory that made these things.

All that effort, so much belief in potions and gadgets. None of it would ever be an effective substitute for a drink, a good laugh and a bag of chips afterwards. Rumour had it that the dildoes were based on plaster-casts taken from famous porn stars. Super Dong, Invader, Rectifier, Climactor Vibe, Large Strap-On; they had awesome names, redolent of Hollywood heroism, but they were as convincing as false teeth, and looked as pinky, waxy and plastic too. It was men who were buying them, supposedly on behalf of their women, as an anniversary treat, perhaps. Didn't they have pricks of their own? Or were they hooked on copy-cat sex, something they'd seen in a porn film, wielding their prosthetics, trying to convince themselves that they were The Tamer, but having as much fun as a gynaecologist with a hangover.

God knows who the inflatable women were modelled on: the pictures in the ad were of real women, soft and cuddly in lacy black lingerie. The woman who emerged from the box was creased and flabby and sad, as cold as yesterday's snot. Her pubes were as convincing as Ronald McDonald's wig and her eyes were fixed on infinity. The whole ensemble was too spooky. To need comfort like this a man must have reached the nadir of sexual melancholy.

Men joked like hell about all this stuff. Suicide would have been the honourable alternative to admitting to buying it. But someone was making Cupid rich. No one really knew what the next man was up to in his bedroom.

Cupid offered a mini-library of books. *The Penis* – 'Renowned sex doctor Dick Richards tells how YOU can have a bigger cock in just six weeks with his proven exercises.' *How to Find and Stimulate Her G-Spot* – 'An incredibly descriptive book that shows you in very sexy photos how to penetrate a woman to really deep levels.' Even *Seven Steps to Psychic Mind Control* – 'Once you incorporate the principles detailed in this book you'll find gorgeous women at your beck and call, always waiting to satisfy your desires.'

The books appealed to the hobbyist in every man, a touching belief that everything could be solved by looking in a manual. Love was merely a technique that could be mastered in easy steps. Cure your baldness, develop iron muscle, extend your prick, get any woman you want. And these were purchased by the same men who made snidey jokes about women car drivers and the shopping habits of their wives.

Despite its looming presence in the world of marital aids, Cupid's new HQ wasn't much bigger than a broom cupboard. In fact, until recently, that's exactly what it had been. Rich landed the task of getting it ready, shifting brooms and cans of Jeyes Fluid down to an even murkier location in the basement. Large spiders, scurrying away from his flapping duster, caused panic amongst the office arachnophobes. But Janice was on hand to save them, thwacking the brave scurriers into oblivion with a rolled-up *Fiesta*.

'Horrible bastards. I hate 'em.'

What a waste. Someone somewhere could have used that in a magic potion! Men had been looking for the sure-fire sex recipe since the year dot. Bull's testicles, rhino horns, bat's blood, stallion's foreskins (pickled), powdered Egyptian mummy – the more gruesome the ingredients the better. If someone had started a rumour that bulldog sperm did the business, punters would have been knocking back pints of it. Dogs would go missing. At a run-down farm somewhere they'd be wanking them off into test-tubes.

One of the tabloids had just done an exposé on Pepé Gomez, a Majorcan spiv who'd been flogging 'Genuine Spanish Fly' at £1 a time to British holidaymakers. Their hopes of giving the local señoritas a thrill were dashed when they got back and opened the tightly corked jars to find a dead fly. Following complaints, police raided Pepé's home and found hundreds of jars and several cans of fly-spray. Pepé claimed the flies were 'novelty souvenirs'. Fined a token £5 for having no pedlar's licence, the next day he was back on the streets.

'He sells exactly what he offers,' said a local cop. 'The worst that can happen is a small fine. Or maybe he gets a punch on the nose.'

Spanish Fly had a reputation. But few people knew that it was really powdered-beetle remains. It gave a man a bone-hard erection by causing severe irritation of the urinary tract. Every bit as lethal as arsenic or strychnine (also regarded by some adventurers as an aphrodisiac!) it had to be calibrated with pharmaceutical precision, not shovelled in with a teaspoon. A nasty death could result from the slightest overdose.

Male culture is based on hearsay, ring-fenced by all kinds of silly myths like Spanish Fly; a belief in magic elixirs and sure-fire techniques. Dynamite information, passed on in whispers. Even the humble potato was reputed to possess such powers when it was first introduced to Elizabethan England. And at school kids sidled up with hot tips. What you were supposed to do, walking along with a girl, was get your finger above her palm and move it round-and-round-the-garden style. Apparently it had a devastating effect. The girl's stomach fluttered, her legs buckled. She'd pull you into the nearest private place, desperate for the feel of your erection inside her.

Today the ingredients are no less daft, but in the West a marketing slant has been attached. The products have been given pseudo-scientific names. Dressed up in clever packaging, there are potions to get things going, pills to slow things down, lotions to maintain erections for hours. Love Lube, Orgasmovite, Erectovite, Sex Sugar, Champion Stud, Action Spray, Stallion Delay Cream, Pleasure Pearls, Female Bliss Cream; the trade has a sleazy poetry all of its own. Cupid even had a special nightcap guaranteed to bring on sexy dreams.

Guaranteed? Legally, healthwise, there were few safeguards. Companies like Cupid knew that fear of ridicule would stop anyone making a fuss. If the products failed to deliver: tough! Even if Erectovite and Pleasure Pearls came within the scope of the Trades Descriptions Act, who was going to make a fuss? No marital-aids consumer group existed to lobby for fair treatment.

Janice was furious. 'I can't get in the bloody toilet now. That fat cow's wedged behind the fucking door!'

The fat cow in question was Bridget the Midget, a five-foot-nothing roly-poly who'd decided to cash in on her size by becoming a model. Bridget was a naked freak. Men marvelled at freakiness. Ten times better when it was a woman. What a laugh they'd have in the garages and site huts.

'Look at them fucking tits, Ken! They'd fucking suffocate yer! Give us a chance.'

Massive mammaries, titanic tits, big boobs; men never miss a chance to marvel. It's passed off as lusty appreciation, but it's always looked more like spiteful pleasure at the burdens women have to hump around. With such handicaps women never catch men up. Boobs. Mistakes. Some men look on smugly, as if one half of the world's population has been condemned to wear comic red noses.

Maybe that's why some men doubly revile tomboyish women with manageable mammaries. Tits have to be on show, not only in the girlie mags, but every single day in the tabloids. Page Three isn't about eroticism or fanciability, it's merely an unsubtle reminder of the status quo.

Geoff came running with his screwdriver. The door was removed and Bridget rescued. She tried to laugh it off, but it was no joke to her.

This was pornography of a different sort. Nothing to do with the pictorial *frisson* of nudity, but a cruel, voyeur mentality that should have died out with the Victorians. Sadly, it was still alive. It took the smile off my face. The dirty letters and the bad-taste jokes I could handle, but my hackles rose at any suggestion of cruelty or unfairness. Maybe the feminists were right: I was underpinning an unforgivable status quo. Was it right that anyone's daughter or mother should have to do this stuff for their daily loaf?

The story became part of the office folklore. Poor Bridget, she died a couple of years later, lampooned, mocked, as much a freak as the Elephant Man. (I'd been in the cinema with Carole for that one and the audience had burst into spontaneous weeping at the end. I'd never heard anything like it. They would have done the same for Bridget, surely.) She passed away in her sleep, her biggest memorial some tacky pictures. Yet I knew someone would have cared for her. Our readers weren't all spiteful wankers, some of them were lonesome gents who would have bought her chocolates, courted her, loved her.

I'd not seen Linda since my weekend in Leicester. She'd sent a couple of letters, to which I replied as indifferently as I could. But cruelty wasn't part of my arsenal. And Linda wasn't letting go so easily. She'd booked into a hotel on the fringes of Belsize Park and telephoned to tell me.

'Come and see me some time,' she begged, in a terrible Mae West pastiche.

The weather was warm, my hormones were flexing, I

couldn't resist. Being cooped up with Elaine in that tiny room was doing my head in. An afternoon in a hotel room sounded like an ideal getaway. Just one more time and then I'd tell her.

'Hotel' in this case was a genteel euphemism. Locals knew it better as a hostel for the homeless. Men sat on the steps with cans of Tennent's, babies wailed from unidentified rooms. At the jokingly entitled 'Reception', a woman with a fag directed me to a room on the second floor. Linda sat on the bed reading *The Stage*.

We had sex, on top of the bedding. I enjoyed it, but I wished I hadn't.

By the time we finished we were both covered in sweat and Linda was coated in little brown hairs from the rough blanket. She looked like some kind of freak-show woman.

I'd got myself in too deep. How would I ever free myself? What if she threatened suicide? By having sex I'd cemented our link. 'Casual sex' was a worse euphemism than hotel. The catchphrase was empty and dishonest. At the end of the day, there was no such thing.

I had to go, I said. Elaine would have my tea ready and there'd be a row if I didn't turn up. I promised to meet Linda in the pub at eight o'clock.

And there I was. But at ten to eight Elaine unexpectedly popped in to join me. She fancied a change from watching TV. I sat with her, sipping my beer, waiting for the inevitable to happen. The locals who knew us smiled indulgently. We were popular with the middle-agers; the perfect young couple. If any of them had known what I'd been doing two hours earlier they'd have spat in my face.

Linda came in, bought a shandy, looked around eagerly, half-smiling for when she caught sight of me. The smile vanished. With admirable disdain she sat down at the opposite end of the bar. She looked at me. Not with hatred, but melancholy. One more shit of a man who couldn't be trusted. But I wanted to be trusted. I couldn't bear to think of myself being classified in the same box of insects as all the other cads. I only just stopped myself from joining her. So what if it caused aggro, wasn't that better than this hypocrisy?

I didn't have to. Linda finished her drink and departed with dignity. Elaine looked up as she passed, only from idle curiosity. She had no idea who the woman was.

Cupid offered Galaxy employees a 15 per cent discount on products. Trevor was always willing to lay on a demonstration in the hope of a sale. We cruelly encouraged him, but only for the entertainment. Even if anyone in the office used marital aids, they'd hardly want Trevor or the rest of Galaxy to know about it. You'd feel as if Trevor was in the bedroom with you, hovering with a salesman's smile, ready with advice on the correct use of the company products.

Depending on his audience his sales pitch ranged from pseudo-scientific to downright crude. Flexing an Ecstasy Probe – 'pliable yet satisfyingly firm' – he was quite shameless: 'Come on, girls, we know you all use them.'

'Fuck off!'

Janice was mortally offended, but Trevor carried on, unperturbed.

'This one's a winner, believe me. The *crème de la crème* of dildoes. Life-like, real-feel. Soft for comfort. Firm for penetrating pleasure. Specially tapered head for easy insertion.'

'Dirty bastard. He needs it inserting up his bloody backside.'

Oddly, with the males, Trevor was much more coy.

'Look lads, we all know the dangers of Aids. We don't want to risk the well-being of our loved ones.'

Coloured condoms were quite enough for some people, though I couldn't see the thrill of disguising your cock as a courgette. Trevor's condom selection was a revelation. Coloured, ribbed, grooved and bobbled, they came in flavours too, from simple strawberry to lager and lime.

In my teenage days condoms were harder to get hold of than booze. Rumour had it that Ces's was worth a visit. A vaguely Fagin-like figure, Ces owned a shop which was a hang-out for all kinds of yobs and hard cases. One attraction was that he'd sell single fags – one fag and two matches for 3p. And for those yobs who'd graduated from fags to sex he sold Durex. If you didn't have cash he'd take a hundred No. 6 coupons. None of us had yet met a girl willing to go that far but we'd buy a Durex anyway, just to hold it between finger and thumb and make out it was destined to get burned up during a hot shag. That it just got masturbated in or used as a water bomb was a secret we kept to ourselves.

A new Cupid line was the pheromone spray, a handy aerosol version of male sexual scent. It worked, according to the ads in *Fiesta*, on a 'subliminal level'. The spray was a 'formula for instant sexcess'; it provided 'spray-on sex appeal'. But it did more than simply turn someone on: any woman getting so much as a whiff would be unable to contain her urges. Simpering virgins were transmogrified into raving nymphos who sent your fly-buttons popping across the room in their indecent haste for sex.

Trevor was so keen to prove it he volunteered to spray himself. 'Proof of the pudding, lads. You watch 'em flock.'

He lurked in the foyer, doing his best to look casual. We watched, but our female colleagues were noticeably reluctant to do any flocking. Not that the smell wasn't noticed – it had a devastating effect on at least one female.

'That Trevor's got a real bad case of BO,' Janice said. 'These fat bastards don't wash enough, that's the trouble. Can't bloody reach properly for a start. All that sweat gets caught up in the flab . . .'

*   *   *

Ever wondered what really happens between
randy young couples alone behind closed
doors? Listen in to the arousing sounds of
these thrusting and throbbing lovers, privately
recorded for your pleasure. Wet, hungry, erotic

and breathless . . . hear these men and women enjoy themselves again and again. Each of our audio tapes is a collection of uninhibited ACTUAL SOUNDS of lovemaking. Real couples making love and enjoying a variety of erotic pleasures. These PRIVATE recordings feature as many as ten different couples in each hour-long tape. Treat yourself now!

Another line was a series of audio-cassettes with titles like *Young and Shameless*, *Student Sex Party* and *Juicy Pleasures*. Instead of buying them from his usual supplier, Trevor had sussed out how easy it was to make them himself. All you needed to do was get a decent tape recorder, a couple of female volunteers and a few bottles of Liebfraumilch to loosen them up, then set up some mikes in the studio. Despite the less than perfect acoustics and the lousy scripts, there were several props that could be used to good effect, like a bed whose springs could be boinged with vigour:

MALE: Bet you've never had one bloke between the two of you before.

TINA: No, but we're quick to learn.

MALE: My prick's big enough for you both to lick.

PAM: Mmmm, it certainly is.

(Slurp slurp, mmmm, slurp, slurp, sigh.)

Mmmm, come on, Tina, get a taste of this.

MALE: Aargh! That's it, girls. Oooh, you randy cows.

(Slurp, slurp, gobble, chew.)

Now, come on, Pam, bend over. That's it.

(Groan. Intake of breath.)

Feel good, does it?

(Sound of mattress. Sighs.)

The girls could hardly keep a straight face. And all the time, none of them had moved from their microphones.

*   *   *

We guessed something was going on. Exactly what, no one knew. Rumours abounded. Janice, always good for a theory, reckoned Russell had got Aids. 'Serves him right, sex maniac bastard.' Amongst his post she'd seen a big brown envelope with a Swiss stamp – obviously a brochure for one of those shady private clinics, she opined.

Poor Russell. Loyal employees (what few there were) sat crying into their tea, thinking of him jacked up in bed, drained of his lifeblood, crumpled like an old carrier bag. Cynics amongst us didn't really care. We enjoyed the break. But the end-of-term anarchy was short-lived.

It didn't take long for the truth to emerge. It wasn't Russell who was buggered, but the company itself. *Fiesta* still topped Britain's girlie mag top ten (a neck ahead of Paul Raymond's *Escort*) and *Knave* held on to its middling position, but somehow things had gone badly wrong. Rumour had it that the printers were owed £250,000. The taxman wanted several backdated slices of the pie. Even the window cleaners hadn't been paid. There'd been fifteen good years, but the net was closing in.

'What's so fucking funny about that?'

Despite Dennis's public relations dictum, I was fed up with nutters. Colin grinned as I crashed the receiver back into its cradle: I was getting as bad as Janice. He didn't know it was because of him. His new-born son was in hospital and I was upset about it.

Colin didn't want our sympathy. Fucking office clichés, the chuntering of old women. His kid was ill, but what the fuck did we care? How could we feel the agony? Maybe he was right about some of them, but I did care. I didn't have children, but I wanted to. I often imagined the children Elaine and I might have – heartstoppingly beautiful little girls. Women would watch us in the park and cluck admiringly. My girls would be tall and slender and elegant. They'd go to Cambridge, become actresses or barristers. Their daddy would always make sure no one like Dennis or Jim Stone would stand watching while they had to take off their clothes for money.

But that family dream seemed to be fading. We'd talked that way for a while, about getting married, buying a house, having a family. But it seemed more and more unlikely. I'd not heard anything from Linda since that day at the hotel. Elaine and I moved from the bedsit in Belsize Park to a flat in Kilburn. For the first time we had a double bed, more room to manoeuvre. I'd given her a load of money and she'd bought all the things a couple might need – saucepans, towels, crockery. But it was too late to start playing the perfect couple, too many things had happened.

I made a half-hearted attempt to blame the work. Daily exposure to nakedness had jaded my appetite, made me an addict for novelty. Working behind the bar I'd made myself sick with longing for Elaine, daren't even imagine the stupendous privilege of ever seeing her naked, making love, sharing a life. But my head had got so stuffed with nudity, so stuffed with the way men made sex into sleazy bravado that I'd gone right off it. It was an industrial injury, an occupational hazard of the most tragic proportions.

It was impossible to switch off completely. Snatches of letters floated about inside my head, images of other girls with legs akimbo. Halfway through making love an image flashed through my mind, followed by some office worry, something really mundane. And in no time you were thinking about the office instead of enjoying yourself. It was a total washout. You came, but not with the wonderful ecstasy you'd been used to.

Bullshit! Who was I kidding? I was the sole culprit. The mags and my work may have played a small part, but in the end it was the insistent itch for adventure, the biological imperative. Evolution had made us into ruthless fucking machines and however hard we tried, we were only human, we couldn't escape our programming.

*   *   *

Then Russell suddenly reappeared, large as life, eyes owl-bright behind his yellow specs. Trailing in his wake came five gents in suits and ties. Awkward, ill-at-ease, they stood around blinking like workmen on a day off. They did odd things – jabbing typewriter keys, testing hole-punches, peering into boxes of paperclips, studying the holiday rota – anything, it seemed to avoid looking interested in the piles of girlie mags or talking to the staff.

'Top blokes from the printer's,' someone muttered. Word quickly went round: these were our new bosses. Russell had gone and sold them the whole caboodle. The deal was something like: wipe out the debt, give me an extra £100,000 and the whole lot's yours – *Fiesta, Knave, Video World*, the typewriters, the paperclips, and all the idle fuckers who work there.

They'd got themselves a goldmine. But blimey:

> Imagine my horror when I looked into my hus-
> band's briefcase for a pen and found it full of
> sex magazines. I feel sickened and betrayed.
> Our marriage can never be the same . . .

If their wives disapproved of dirty books and the beasts who read them, what on earth were they going to say when their hubbies brought a whole porno empire home? It wasn't as if it could be hidden in the wardrobe or anything. They'd be in deep shit.

Still, when the wives saw their share dividend they'd soon lighten up. 'My husband is in printing. My son is a sales director' – that's all they had to say. No need to mention bare tits and winking vaginas to anyone. After all, it wasn't their daughters showing off their bits, nor their sons making up those filthy stories. They were not corrupted, they merely banked the proceeds. It wasn't porn, not at a distance, just one small part of a portfolio of business interests.

Why did I think girlie mags were beyond the pale? True,

no one with any pretensions to decent middle-class values could be caught reading one, but as a business it was as legitimate as stationery or biscuit-making. No doubt High Street banks and lawyers and accountants were involved, drawing up loan agreements and contracts. But would the girls at the bank who totted up the pennies realize it was all coined from porn? Would they really care? Who'd dare protest? No one. At the end of the day, the pornographer's pound was just as good when it came to paying off the mortgage and buying the groceries.

'Don't drink too much wine,' warned various gloommongers. 'It'll leak out the stab wounds in your back.'

We were on our way to Essex for a look around the printer's HQ. Those with cars made their own way, the rest of us piled into the company minibus for the trip.

Aperitifs, entrées, steaks the size of school satchels, gorgeous sweets, liqueurs – they gave us the works. Despite the warnings, those who usually existed on Heinz spaghetti or take-away pizzas were determined to make the most of it. Our hosts touched our shoulders in a matey way, making sure everything was to our satisfaction.

But there were disturbing hints. Wasn't Essex a wonderful county they gushed. No hustle or aggro like London. You woke to the sound of birdsong. Your money went half as far again. Barrett had built some lovely new houses. They had good contacts on the council for those who preferred to rent.

We were all sworn to secrecy. It wasn't just their wives they were scared of. These men were probably cornerstones of the local Rotary Club, the Chamber of Trade or the Conservative Association. If it came out they were making money from porn there'd be a scandal the like of which had never been known in the shires.

Russell was off. He'd got himself a bolt-hole in the South of France. On his last day, taking some of his gear down to his Mercedes he narrowly missed aquaplaning through a small lake of primrose yellow emulsion. Geoff had been at it again.

'I'll kill him!'

Geoff wandered into view, Bambi innocently straying into the sights of a hunting rifle. Behind the security door we jostled for a front-row view. Janice put all calls on hold.

'Sorry, Russell,' said Geoff. He smiled apologetically and waved a J-Cloth in the air. 'I was just going to clean it up.'

It wasn't so much the spill that enraged Russell, but Geoff's wooden-topped optimism. He was going to mop up five litres of paint with a J-Cloth?

'Get your fucking cards, Geoff.'

'Yes, Russell. I'll just get this cleared up before I go, shall I?'

'Fuck the fucking paint! Just get out of my building before I get a High Court injunction . . .'

Geoff looked ready to burst into tears, not appreciating the joke. He edged round the pool of paint and went downstairs. Russell, being fatter, couldn't edge so easily and went down to his car leaving a trail of primrose yellow footprints. A torn newspaper page fluttered by. Russell grabbed it and wiped his soles with it. Then he got into the Mercedes and drove away, with strips of the *Daily Mirror* still sticking to his shoes.

'Bye, then,' snarled Janice, flashing a V-sign through the upstairs window. 'Fat bastard.'

New management were trading on everyone's toes, making up new rules, scrutinizing every cheque and invoice, demanding to know who was who, who did what. A red triangle sign should have been set up by the front door: Caution, Backstabbers At Work. There were old scores to settle. Without Russell Gay's patronage some people were doomed. Dennis for one. He'd made the mistake of telling our new bosses how to run things – a reasonable enough thing to do, since he'd been in the business so long. But they probably remembered the man who'd given them so much grief, nit-picking about the tiniest printing errors, forever ringing them up to complain that such and such a picture was more like 69 per cent cyan than the 70 per cent he'd specified.

Dennis's fate was decided by a majority vote of the board, but it was Russell Gay's long-suffering managing director who rushed to volunteer for the job of telling him. We couldn't hear the conversation, but we could see it. He handed the bags to Dennis, told him to empty his drawers and leave the building.

If they expected Colin to be chuffed at being made editor they were mistaken. Our lives as assistants were slack and cosy. Neither of us ever wanted the hassle of being top man.

There were perks. Without Dennis breathing down his neck Colin was able to spend longer and longer at lunch, leaving me virtually in charge of day-to-day running and boosting my salary by asking me to write articles and fillers.

But I was bored with it all. Bored and under stress. Elaine made it plain she was going. She'd had enough. It was crunch time for both of us. Instead of hanging on to some constancy, I decided to go for broke and handed in my notice. Colin didn't want me to go, but I'd made my mind up. Two years was enough. For a while I'd been over the moon, but it hadn't taken me long to wise up. A factory is just a factory and a worker still a worker, no matter how they're dressed up. What difference was there between turning out a daily quota of Wellington boots and bashing out two dozen readers' letters, six girlie blurbs and three confessions?

The whip round yielded enough for them to buy me a pen and a Marks and Spencer jumper. There was also a big farewell card. The art room had made a neat job of fitting a mugshot of me on to the body of a reader's wife. So cleverly done that it gave me the creeps. So, this was how I'd look if I'd been a woman: not a pretty, blonde undergraduate swinging down the street in blue jeans, but a lipsticked housewife wearing shiny black and crimson knickers and a ridiculous pout. How utterly symbolic: this identikit tart was just what I'd become.

With the transsexual ID card tucked under my arm, I walked down the stairs and set off back down Belsize Road. I had no regrets.

A week later Belsize Park had its annual festival. Elaine's kid brother came up to help her with her bags. Up on the dais, a reggae band chugged their way through hits that ought to have had me sobbing: 'No Woman No Cry', 'Is This Love That I'm Feeling?' But I refused to make a big deal out of it. The sun was blazing, the beer flowing, the square full of pretty girls. This was a trial separation, a breathing space. Elaine would soon be back.

Suddenly she was gone. The carnival was over, the pavements strewn with cracked plastic beer glasses and jettisoned hot dogs. I walked back down the road. I'd managed to get a room back in 14a, Babs' old place, the bedsit with the curse – the loner's room, the nutter's room. Yet it now resembled an ideal home exhibit, slightly squashed in maybe, but I must have been the only person in bedsitland who had a twenty-four-piece dinner service (Country Harvest design) and four spanking new saucepans all of my own!

6   Starting *Razzle*

With summer halfway through already, I resolved to enjoy what was left of it. Fully equipped for a doss (fags, beer, Sony Walkman, *Times* crossword), I took up my pose on the tiled steps of 14 Belsize Park Gardens. Since leaving school ten years previously I'd gone through the job/no-job cycle so many times it was never going to make that much difference. Money wasn't a problem – unless you wanted to be pedantic and weigh up my £500 savings against the £800 I owed Barclaycard. All kinds of people stopped by, and so long as they didn't represent a High Street bank it was fine by me. We chatted, smoked, swigged, frowned over cryptic clues. I felt as at ease with life as a yokel leaning on a five-bar gate.

Then the sun went in. One day the steps were hot enough to fry an egg on, the next I just felt stupid, a guy in shorts sitting on a cold tombstone. Back indoors, alone with my typewriter, the dreams of writing-fame faded in and out like voices on short-wave, loud and clear one second, squashed flat in howling static the next. I had to admit it: I was lazy, stupid, talentless and totally lacking in self-discipline. What right had I to waste so much paper? In distant gulags there were prisoners who'd have swapped a week's bread rations for a single scrumpled sheet from my bin.

The money dwindled. Boring Rich Tea replaced yummy choc chip cookies. The windowsill in front of my desk looked like a bombed-out airfield, littered with wrecked fighter planes. They were only the obstinate corpses of dead flies, but sitting, staring, I half-expected to see tiny men in goggles and white silk scarves climb down from their cockpits.

Worse than bad housekeeping, worse than poverty, I missed Elaine. Photos of her were pinned and Blu-Tacked to every available surface – a shrine to failure. I paced my room, clawing the crumpled mask of my face, snivelling back tears – all done to music, like some fat tenor hamming it up in a tragic opera. Bloody Neil Young! That miserable Canadian strummer! Why had I chosen 'Only Love Can Break Your Heart' as our song? How else to explain, except it was obviously a death wish in song form. Even when I'd first heard it, I'd had a spooky vision: myself several years hence, in a room, something like the one I was in now.

When it came to misery, male culture was all but useless. Tea and sympathy were for sissies. Counselling had too many syllables to be a manly word. From past experience I knew that advice from blokes like Tone and Phil, but echoed even by nice chaps like Guy, came in man-sized chunks, hard to chew but designed to make you a better man in the long run. Treat 'em mean and keep 'em keen. Give no quarter. Fuck 'em and forget 'em. Fuck 'em if they don't appreciate you. Letting women make you cry was frowned upon.

But I didn't want a pep-talk about pulling myself together, not letting the side down. I hadn't given up. I wrote to Elaine and begged. I rang her up and begged. I caught a rattling diesel train to Henley and yelled my apologies above the crackling of a cellophane-wrapped bouquet. Kindness, gallantry, romance; these were my new watchwords. She agreed to come for a pizza. I even thought that getting her to share a plate of garlic bread was a positive sign. When our fingertips touched greasily in a play for the last slice, I gave her a fond smile and begged her to take it.

Marriage was the trump card. The papers were full of ads for Barrett homes in Englishy places like Marlow,

Bourne End and Cookham, neat nests for newly-weds, cookers and carpets included. I'd commute up to London every morning, commute back every night, live a slippers 'n' telly lifestyle well away from temptation.

Elaine erupted. Wasn't I listening? If her little sister could spell antidisestablishmentarianism, why couldn't I grasp a modest two-syllable word like 'finished'?

'You've got to forget me. You're not bad-looking. You're kind and brainy. There's hundreds of women who'd love to go out with you.'

I didn't understand. If I was so wonderful, what was the problem? Why did women say these awful things, impossible conundrums, designed to send men mad?

Beer followed beer until I was way over. I missed the train back to London and had to stay over. But I hadn't drunk enough to forget. Lying miserably on the Z-bed downstairs, I fidgeted so much that the back legs folded up, pitching my head to the floor. Concussed, I slept. After breakfast I left. I never saw that lovely kitchen again.

Passing the Pizza Hut I glanced in and saw the cellophaned bouquet, still under our table, where it had been forgotten . . .

Back in Belsize Park, waking in the night, my only prop was to bite my toe-nails (my fingernails were long gone). Curled up like some hobbledehoy foetus, I sat ripping off slivers of nail and spitting them out on to the carpet. I dreamt up a last ludicrous gesture. I would ask that nutter from the attic flat to kill me, remove my head, put it in a cardboard box and leave it on Elaine's doorstep alongside the milk and eggs. Opened, it would be the final reproach. Her screams would echo across the town. I could see it all unfolding like a film scene. I could see the posters, forties Hollywood style: 'His Love Was Deeper Than She Knew.' Then the funeral. My head, neatly stitched back to the rest of me, lies back on a silken pillow with a 'told you so' smirk, a tribute to the embalmer's art. Elaine weeps into a lacy handkerchief, her mum says: 'He would have made such a good husband.' Morbid nonsense, but I found it strangely comforting.

One morning, Dennis rang. Since getting the boot he'd been busily touting his CV around, but without much success. Finally he'd struck lucky: Paul Raymond had hired him to start a new magazine. A salary was important, of course, but the big bonus for Dennis was revenge. Sweet revenge. The new magazine would be set up in direct competition with *Fiesta*. Dennis was determined to chase their tail to the top of the circulation charts. Even the title – *Razzle* – sounded like a loud raspberry to those po-faced Essex printers.

Dennis courted me with embarrassing zeal. I had talent, we were a proven team, I was an excellent pornographer, he wanted me on board. The flattery almost worked. Then I remembered the nit-picking arguments, the paranoia, the dirty looks after the long lunches. Staying in was doing me no good, I knew: I needed people around me, money in the bank, the distractions of a routine. But not that routine.

I told him I'd think about it, but only to get him off my back.

During my two years at *Fiesta* I'd dutifully snipped out all my cuttings, pasted them neatly in a book, annotated them with dates and issue numbers. That's what ambitious journalists did. Now, sitting and re-reading them I realized what a wasted exercise it had been. Even though I'd trimmed away as much of the flesh as possible, pasted the paper down so no one would see the tits on the reverse, I knew they were worse than useless. However clever, funny or well-crafted, it was still porn. No decent editor would sit there reading a girlie blurb or an 'I Confess' without making immediate judgements: rapist, child molester, at the mildest a leather fetishist and practised sexual harasser. How could anyone hire a person like me? As soon as my secret past was uncovered, no woman would feel safe walking by my desk. These were PC days. There'd be union meetings, calls for my sacking.

Where else could I go? What was the point in bashing my head against a brick wall when I had a job for the asking? No interview. No new routines to learn. No need for awkward explanations.

So, in the end, I rang Dennis and agreed. I'd have to sort the rest of my life out at some later date.

'Paul Raymond?' Tone and Phil were mightily impressed. They'd heard of him. Everyone had. Unlike the reclusive Russell Gay, Paul Raymond was famous, a larger-than-life figure who ran world-famous sex shows and had a string of top-class girlfriends. He even looked OK, not fat and sinister, but an amiable cove whose moustache and hippy hairstyle lent him a reassuring air; not an evil exploiter of women, but a ringmaster who gave men a glimpse of sexual heaven.

'Doesn't he shag that Fiona Richmond?' said Phil.

'That was bloody years ago!' snapped Tone. 'He's shagging somebody else nowadays.'

Raymond Towers, as wags dubbed the HQ of the empire, is a warren of offices at the back of the old Paramount Theatre on the corner of Archer Street. Probably the dullest thoroughfare in Soho, it's more of a wide alley than a decent street. A pub at each end, a couple of casinos and a newsagent's, that was about it. Apart from the desperate patter of the old tart on the door of its one clip-joint, it held no attractions for punters.

With *Men Only*, *Club* and *Escort* already dug in, the building didn't have much room for another crew. *Razzle*'s first office was no bigger than a generous-sized loo, sparsely equipped with a desk and two old dining chairs, a heavy old typewriter and a Cinzano ashtray, which quickly filled as we struggled to come up with feature ideas. Dennis looked fed up. After being editor of Britain's top girlie mag this was a real bummer. Where was the majestic editor's chair, the loyal secretary with the tea and the direct-line telephone? To operate efficiently, an editor needed to swivel and rock. They needed coffee and someone to bring it in. And they certainly shouldn't have to beg the switchboard girl every time they wanted an outside line!

A chatty type, loath to get mixed up in office politics, I quickly made friends with the editors of *Men Only*, *Club* and *Escort*. Dennis didn't like it, though. Why had I been so long if I was just borrowing Tipp-Ex? Did I need to take cigarettes off rival editors? He'd convinced himself they were out to steal our ideas. The top half of our cubby-hole was frosted glass: every time Dennis saw a blurred shadow he tensed up. Why wasn't it moving? Who was lurking, listening, jotting down notes?

His appeals for proper offices were finally answered. Paul Raymond's son led us round to nearby Brewer Street. From the doorway of No. 6, set back off the pavement between a porn cinema and an off-licence, a dried-up stain of piss ran across to the gutter. Dennis and I followed him up three flights of dank smelling stairs, exchanging looks of alarm when Howard Raymond halted at the door of a derelict room. An office, they'd promised. How dare they try and palm us off with this evil squat?

Still, bad as it looked, we were filled with an urge to make it our own.

Two days later the building echoed with fruity curses as Cockneys in overalls struggled up the same three flights with new desks and filing cabinets. Enthroned in the new editor's chair, Dennis tested it for rockability and swivel-ability. For the first time in weeks he looked happy. 6 Brewer Street would be his fiefdom, a semi-autonomous outpost to the Raymond empire. Everyone here would be under his command, dedicated to *Razzle*, the threat of spies and moles strictly minimal.

We even had our own cleaner, a cheerful one-eyed Jamaican called Leroy. Though I could never understand his babble, his unsquashable good humour made me feel protective. Given his visual handicap we could hardly blame him for leaving one half of everything unpolished. When Dennis wasn't looking I ran round the furniture and wiped away the tell-tale signs.

That was me, always for the underdog. Wasn't I one myself? Dennis had ennobled me as 'Deputy Editor'. No doubt he thought it generous. And, yes, it sounded great. Until you put it in context. At *The Times* or on the *NME* such a title might carry some clout. But Deputy Editor, *Razzle* – how could it be anything more than a joke? People like Tone and Phil were impressed, but I knew the truth: at the end of the day I was still number two in a list of two.

Paul Raymond wasn't going to risk too much cash on this new venture, hence his decision to test the market for a scaled-down 50p version of a girlie mag. With only forty-eight pages *Razzle* would be half the size of its rivals, but Dennis was determined to pack it full of sauce. Starting a magazine from scratch wasn't easy. Even he had never faced that challenge before. For instance, without readers, how could we have readers' letters? One of my first tasks was to bash out some fictitious ones. They came easily enough. I still suffered from mental burn-in. The wires in my brain had been fused. Porn stories were almost second nature: I had the vocabulary and the narrative off-pat and random lines still cluttered up my brain.

A few days after we moved in, from somewhere in the maze of corridors, came the sound of whistling. It was 'O Sole Mio', out of tune and sizzly with spit, and in the half-empty building it sounded quite spooky. It couldn't be the builders since they'd left days ago. Dennis tensed and bit perforations in the tip of his Dunhill.

'Go and see who that is,' he commanded.

I went out, but saw no one. Cautiously, I walked to the end of the unlit corridor. A door banged to somewhere in the gloom and I fled back to the light of the office.

'Must've been a ghost,' I joked.

An hour later we heard the whistling again, a few bars

from *Don Giovanni* this time. Dennis decided to go and look for himself. A minute later he returned, wordless and ashen-faced, and lit another Dunhill.

'Some bugger playing tricks.'

A white figure floated past the door and I felt my bowels shift an inch or two inside me. I looked at Dennis. Dennis looked at me. Shit! The place was haunted.

'Wotcha, my friend.'

Dropping two heavy cardboard boxes on the floor, the ghost fiddled at the huge bunch of keys that jangled from his belt.

'Go and ask him what he's doing,' Dennis snapped. 'We can't have people wandering around the building willy-nilly.'

The ghost poked his head through our doorway and stared round, nodding approval at the spanking new furniture.

'You just moved in? Paul sez he had some guys coming in to start a new mag or something.'

'What's your business up here?' Dennis asked.

'Just popped up for some more ketchup, innit?'

He found the right key and unlocked the blank door next to our office. We stood by, fascinated, as it opened on a tiny room, almost totally occupied by a giant freezer full of kebabs and beefburgers. Above it were shelves stacked with wholesale drums of tomato ketchup, sachets of mustard and packets of paper serviettes.

'It's a fucking restaurant,' muttered Dennis. He picked up a wooden chip fork and looked as if he might launch a *Psycho*-style attack.

Back at his desk, he got on the phone to Archer Street. But it turned out to be all above board. The man ran the food-stall downstairs and was a bona fide tenant of Paul Raymond's, with free access to the building. So he was the greasy bastard responsible for the stink of onions wafting in through the window all day. In vertical terms his counter was only four or five feet away.

'Burger and onions, please, mate.' 'Gizza cold Coke, pal.'
'Doner kebab, no tomatoes.'

Dennis raised his eyes skyward every time the voices
rose to disturb his concentration. Here we were trying to
give birth to a magazine, and we had to share premises with
a swarthy kebab seller who looked like he moonlighted as
a hit-man for the PLO. Not only that, but he was on first
name terms with Paul Raymond. It was so unfair.

I couldn't care less. Instead of suffocating in Raymond
Towers we now had a window on the world. After Kilburn's provincial dullness, Soho was brilliant and upbeat.
The market was virtually under the window, its stalls piled
high with oranges, plums and shiny peppers. There were
barrow boys in blue coats, shame-faced punters, pimps in
sharp suits and backpackers bent under giant rucksacks
wearing ironic expressions in case anyone wondered at
their motives. Around the corner in Wardour Street motorbike messengers swerved and dodged their way through
traffic, while famous faces brushed impatiently past winos,
on their way to lunches with publishers and film-makers.

Prostitutes too were part of the scene. One in particular,
who always stood directly under my window. I never saw
her face, or even her figure, just the Walnut Whip of
lacquered hair and the glowing end of a twig-like
cigarette.

Dennis didn't approve of me standing at the window,
but at least I could warn him if anyone from Archer Street
was coming to check on us. Like the big boss himself.

With his Rolls-Royce, West End penthouse and celebrity
girlfriends, Paul Raymond had all the props. He was the
last of his kind, just the man that popular imagination
demands a porn baron should be. The story has a rags-to-
riches angle too. Paul Raymond started off in showbiz, tour-
ing the country with a mind-reading act bought for £25. It
didn't take him long to twig that the audience were more
interested in his sequinned assistant than the wonders of
telepathy. Telekinesis would only interest these guys when

it could twang off the buckle of a bird's bra-strap! Raymond decided to cash in on their one-track minds by making the shapely girls a central part of his act. Before long he'd made enough to hire premises in Soho. Raymond's Revuebar was an immediate success, financing his move into magazines and property.

The Revuebar is still one of Soho's biggest attractions. Excepting *The Mousetrap* it's probably Britain's longest-running show and its permanent presence lends it an air of respectability. If pornography has any sense of tradition, any desire to have an institution of its own, this would probably be it. The giant illuminated sign has flickered and winked over Soho since the sixties. No doubt at all that this is the centre of Soho (and the world, if the extended claim is to be believed).

RAYMOND'S REVUEBAR
THE WORLD CENTRE OF
EROTIC ENTERTAINMENT

Personal Appearances
of the World's Greatest Names
in Striptease

During the past four decades millions of punters must have stopped and stared at this twinkling neon come-on. Though it could never be officially recognized as a tourist draw, it's as much a part of London as the lights of Piccadilly Circus. And yet, though the Dutch have made a big thing out of sex, the British, historically, have had to pretend it didn't exist, even when it semaphored its presence with 500 kilowatts of multicoloured light bulbs. (Every now and then Westminster Council would have one of its crackdowns, outlawing porn cinemas or peepshows. The next week the same premises would be in use with a new entertainment, revamped as a porno bookshop. It came down in the end to lawyers pitting themselves against lawyers, opening and closing loopholes with comical timing worthy of a Whitehall farce. Nothing changed.)

Out of that dawdling multitude of light bulbs, I doubt if anyone has ever noticed the gaps between the joists that held up the sign. Behind those pigeon-shitted iron ledges lay a dusty window, from which *Razzle* staff with nothing better to do looked out in the hope of a laugh. And Soho always had plenty of laughs to offer: Americans in trousers of the craziest tartan; Japanese badly in need of dentistry and fashionable specs; dithering punters who thought people actually cared whether they went in a dirty book-shop or not. Guilt probably made these punters think God was watching and scowling, but there was only us, drinking coffee and spluttering with voyeuristic laughter.

Paul Raymond wasn't merely a figure of myth. With his fur coat, gold chain and gentleman's bag he was a familiar part of the Soho scene, a man of the people. All the barrow boys had a cheery 'Wotcha, Paul' whenever he passed.

Our first face-to-face encounter was in the coffin-sized lift at Archer Street. Raymond had been three steps behind me, but I pretended ignorance and let the doors close on him. Let him walk! What small talk could I possibly make with a man who was not only my boss but a multimillion-aire as well?

At the last minute, in the interests of diplomacy (and job security), I pressed Door Hold and stood aside to let him in. How was I getting on in Brewer Street, he asked. OK I said, except that no coffee had been provided, hence my foraging trip. As soon as the lift doors slid open he was on the case, demanding to know why we'd been left coffee-less. A minion was dispatched to the store cupboard and I left with as many packets of coffee as I could carry. Despite this obvious burden, the crone at the clip-joint parroted her spiel as I passed. Were these people stupid as well as ugly? Was it likely that a punter would be strolling around Soho with his arms full of Colombian coffee?

In an outward sequence from Paul Raymond's sun circled

Carl Snitcher the legal hawk, John the finance whizz, Nevile Player the maverick editor of Escort. Dennis always felt excluded from this inner circle. And with good cause. In orbital terms, he was a lonely asteroid out around Pluto way.

The Paul Raymond Organization was, in many ways, zanily old-fashioned, staffed by ex-showbiz people. Employees who didn't have their wages paid directly into the bank were required to form a queue at a room in the attic regions of the Paramount. Here, in return for a dotted-line signature, two fussy old gents handed out the wages in small brown envelopes.

The switchboard was slightly more up-to-date and certainly run more politely than the one at Galaxy. Lavinia, the resting actress in charge, rarely told anyone to fuck off but merely claimed not to understand their suggestions. Whenever she was off sick (quite often given the strains of the job) Paul Raymond's chauffeur grudgingly allowed himself to be press-ganged. Protocol went out of the window then. All callers, nutty or otherwise, were put straight through.

Dennis insisted that *Razzle* needed a Readers' Wives page. But again the same dilemma: no readers, no wives. Why not borrow a few snaps from the editor of *Escort*, I suggested. Dennis exploded: not only did he not want to be indebted to 'those bastards in Archer Street' he'd be damned if he'd insult *Razzle*'s readers-to-be by palming them off with *Escort*'s rejects. Instead, why didn't I go on a recruiting drive in Belsize Park?

'You know all the local women. What about those two au pairs you told me about – they'd like to earn a bit of pin money, wouldn't they?'

I wasn't so sure. Pitusa and Maria were good Spanish girls. Poor yes, but as haughty as flamenco dancers. Did Dennis really imagine they'd take their knickers off for a few quid? I suggested it could be dangerous: one phone call and they'd have a brother on the next Iberia flight, stiletto newly sharpened to avenge the insult.

'What about those girls from the drama school, then?' Dennis sounded increasingly desperate. 'We need some extroverts. They'd get their knickers off quick enough if Ken Russell rang them up.'

That much was true. Rachel and Nicola and Eva would happily strip for a part in a Channel Four film. But going nude for art's sake was one thing, doing it to titillate the lorry drivers and garage mechanics of Britain quite another. Anyway, I didn't think they looked the part. Readers' Wives usually came from Macclesfield and Newton Abbot and Paisley. However pretty, they always carried an unmistakable provincial air about them. They were certainly of different stock than these zany students with rich daddies. Rachel, for instance, was a pretty Hampstead elfin who hung around in the local wine bars and cafés in the hope of becoming a Martin Amis groupie.

Since Guy knew Rachel better than I did, I set him the task of persuading her.

'Go nude in a dirty mag?' She gasped at the audacity. 'So all those perves can look at me and wank off? What do you think I am, Guy?'

'There's fifty quid in it,' he said. 'And I'll be taking the pictures. It's for Readers' Wives, so it doesn't have to look too swish.'

'Readers' Wives? Do you want me to bring a feather duster and an apron, then?' Already she was relishing the chance to do some dressing up.

Next day, at the flat, while Guy threaded a film into the camera I'd lent him, she rubbed her lovely hands in front of the one-bar electric fire that made a miserable attempt to warm the place, moaning about the cold.

'Never mind. It'll make your nipples stand up. Nick's readers like that sort of thing.'

My readers?

'He's not staying, is he?' said Rachel.

'I just want to explain the kind of poses they like,' I said. 'Then I'll make a coffee. I'm not interested in your nudity.'

'Why not?' Rachel bridled.

'I've seen it all before.'

The truth – and how sad it was. Years ago, before *Fiesta*, I'd have made any excuse to hang around. But now it was all so mundane. When I thought back, to how excited I'd got over an old copy of *Outdoor Leisure*, with its black and white nudists at play, it seemed like the spice had gone out of it all.

I retired to the kitchen, put the kettle on and sat down on the stool to pass the time with a crossword. I made Guy and Rachel a coffee, but when I took it through they'd locked the door. On the other side, it sounded as if someone was having an asthma attack while playing on a trampoline. I felt like knocking, telling Guy to be more professional. I hated him for having so much enthusiasm.

I never told Dennis, but I could have helped out with some pics. I still had some nude pictures of Elaine I'd taken with my new camera. But, no, they were just for me. To look at when she wasn't there. After we'd split up, I'd offered to give them back. Mock gallantry. I was glad when she said she wasn't bothered.

Years later, on the dole, desperate for cash, the thought of selling them crossed my mind again. No one would have been any the wiser and I'd have made a handy £100. Luckily, the moment passed. And I'm glad it did. I'd have regretted it for the rest of my life. Being found out and marked down as a real devious scumbag wasn't what stopped me. No, it was something else. I'd always loved girls for the poetry of their names: she would always be my Elaine of Henley-on-Thames. To see her in *Razzle*, falsely labelled as Tracey of Blackburn, would have made me weep.

One day Dennis asked me to think up a suitable pseudonym for his latest model, a mature woman he hoped would become a *Razzle* favourite. As well as sporting her rubbery nipples and salt and pepper pubes, her middle-age would be touted as a suitable qualification for dispensing advice. Lots of men had a thing about mature women. For some it was simply physical and they'd have swapped a hundred slender beauties for a sagging momma type. For others it was a desperate belief in the advice that older women could offer. Dennis saw it as the perfect combination – an agony aunt who got 'em off.

What's in a name? Quite a lot for some punters, which is why models are rarely, if ever, called Agnes or Ivy or Dot. On the other hand, Cindy, Samantha and Racquel come pre-packed with a sexual CV.

I suggested Sadie Foxx, a name packed with subliminals. Sadie came from the Beatles' 'Sexy Sadie' and also carried a playful hint of sadism. Foxx equalled Foxy, and the ending gave it a double X-certificate feel.

All in all, I was quite pleased with the complex punning. But I'd quite forgotten that the man who'd bought Galaxy and sacked Dennis was called Ron Fox. Any resemblance was purely coincidental, etc. Mr Fox didn't think so. He rang Paul Raymond's office and blew his top: Dennis was using the pages of *Razzle* to take an obvious pop at him. Legal action was threatened, but Paul Raymond stood his ground. Dennis was delighted.

A week later Ivan, the editor of *Knave*, rang me up and asked if I was free for lunch. He wanted a chat about the freelance work I still did for Galaxy – dirty crosswords, picture captions – a useful £100 a month on top of the meagre *Razzle* salary. After a few glasses of Chianti at La Verde Valle, a cosy Italian place with pink tablecloths and waiters in red waistcoats, Ivan plucked up courage to tell me: my services were no longer required. *Fiesta* was changing its image, he said. He'd let me know if there was anything else, etc. Bloody excuses. Because they couldn't get at Dennis or Paul Raymond, the Galaxy bosses had lined me up as the sacrificial goat.

* * *

I still had attacks of the zombies. Most days were OK, I hardly gave Elaine a thought. Then – wham! – I felt utterly lost. A terrible notion took shape: what if I never got over it? The more I toyed with the theory – Perpetual Misery – the more I got myself into a state. Going to work by Tube didn't help, either. Once, I'd loved the Underground, its noise, smells and bustle, but it was no place for a depressed soul. So long as the train kept moving I could think I was going somewhere. When it stopped in the tunnel I wanted to scream. The symbolism was unbearable. The faces of fellow passengers bulged out at me like Hammer horror bogeymen. To avoid freaking, I looked at my newspaper, desperate for distractions – crosswords, football scores, share prices, anything to take my mind off it. Rushing into Leicester Square was rather like an orgasm. And possibly better.

Guy couldn't understand my gloom. Why was I taking it so hard? I should be glad to be free. In his reading, Elaine had made my life a misery, forever checking up on me, showing me up. What about that pint of lager she'd thrown over me in the Belsize Tavern? Or the time she'd gone and sat outside the pub crying and everyone had looked at me like I was the worst shit alive? A cautionary slap would have worked wonders, but I'd left it too late. Now I had to forget her, start afresh. London was jam-packed with women just waiting to be asked. Belsize Park hadn't lost its magic, just me.

I knew he was right. But my confidence had vanished. This was the dilemma. Winning Elaine made my confidence soar, so much I'd kept wanting to keep in practice. Confidence was great, but it only worked when you kept getting feedback.

Spring arrived. Feeling much better, I started walking to work. London in the sunshine is as good as Paris or Copenhagen any day. The view from Primrose Hill never failed to make me appreciate how lucky I was to live in the capital. The baseball games in Regent's Park made me feel London was just the next door village to New York. When I saw the tourists hiking up and down Baker Street with their backpacks I wanted to rush up to them and say, 'Welcome to my town.'

With spring, cornily, came romance, or at least distraction. I'd fallen for a girl called Carol. Tall, slim, pixieish, I sickened for the want of her. Trouble was, she already lived with someone, a pimply youth called Quentin. I hated him. And I hated myself for hating him – he was probably a nice guy. Even if he looked like a wimp, at least he'd had the guts to make a move. Whenever I got a chance I just seized up.

Every Friday at 2 p.m. Carol went to the village launderette. I skived off work and made sure I was there too, my blue bag packed with perfectly clean clothes, roughed up to create the illusion of dirt. This charade didn't come cheap, but I was more than happy to waste £2.50 sending the stuff through a useless cycle of sudsing and spin-drying. Desperate to look casual, I made small-talk about the merits of biological and non-biological powders and went home kicking myself: I'd made no more impression than a grasshopper dancing on an anvil.

Seeing Carol's knickers was the closest I'd ever get. Even that filled me with unendurable jealousy. It wasn't the idea of Quentin having sex with her – what right had I to object? – it was something more tenuous. What made me sick with envy was that he saw her in these knickers, thought next to nothing of it even as she swanned around the flat in her semi-*déshabillé*.

I sent her a Valentine, left bunches of flowers on her doorstep. But what did I expect from such pathetic gestures? Sometimes in the pub we exchanged glances and I fancied that she'd guessed. It wasn't the losing her that hurt, but the kicking I gave myself for not even trying.

There were distractions, like Gitte, the Danish girl who lived upstairs from me. She wanted to see Brighton. I gladly offered to take her. After the usual romantic nonsense – scrunching across the pebbles, laughing in the wind, kissing in the sea-spray – we found a little bistro and got drunk on Muscadet. We caught the last train back to London and she stayed the night.

Considering her Danish upbringing, in a country where pornography was quite open, I was surprisingly coy about telling her what I did. I knew Scandinavians were brought up with a different attitude, but I suspected they looked on the poor Brits and their comic-book titillation with a feeling of pity.

Gitte worked as an auxiliary in the local hospice. What would she do, I asked, if some man begged for a last leg-over before passing on? A flippant question, really, but she answered with ready honesty: yes, sure, she'd give him whatever he wanted. Full sex, if he had the energy, slow pampering oral if he simply wanted to lie back. Who would deserve any less?

I found her charity admirable. Yet I couldn't help detecting a lack of something. Brisk, efficient, eagerly liberal, milking a patient's balls would have meant no more to Gitte than supplying a bedpan or hooking someone up to a saline drip. Would she enjoy it, though? She looked at me stonily. How could you enjoy sex with someone you knew was going to be dead within a couple of weeks?

Then one evening I walked into the Belsize Tavern and Connie was behind the bar. Love at first sight? Hardly. Her presence barely registered. Except for the girls I'd worked with, I'd always deemed chatting up barmaids infra dig, a last resort for sozzled loners who never met girls in any other way. Watching these guys at work was great entertainment, in a cruel, toe-curling way. Every smile was interpreted as a come-on, a light shining into their loneliness. These would-be suitors always drank way too much, since each purchase offered a chance to chat. By ten o'clock the stool they perched on was already swaying dangerously. At around half-past it toppled, with a crash that alerted the whole pub to their hopelessness.

For others, Tone and Phil for instance, the parley was merely reflex. They made smutty comments as casually as they asked for a bag of dry roasted peanuts. It wasn't even chatting up, not in any seriously intended way, for they'd been around long enough to know that few barmaids take their customers seriously. It was a sport, that's all. Men prided themselves on their prowess. And even if they were lousy at it (which they invariably were), they were expected to at least have a go. A favourite game was to get the poor girl to bend down for something below the bar – thereby affording onlookers a good eyeful of boobs.

Since Connie was obviously not from the buxom-wench mould nor the type to stand any nonsense, the usual chatter-uppers didn't bother. I talked to her while she dried glasses, but I had no plan. The idea of asking her out never even occurred to me, until someone else reckoned she fancied me. Disbelieving, I asked her to come to the Pizza Express in Hampstead, certain that she'd refuse.

She accepted eagerly.

I only found out afterwards that Connie had a barstool beau, but he was so shy and retiring that I hadn't even noticed. I'd gone and snatched her away from under his nose and he hadn't even glared, just accepted his defeat and bought another pint. I didn't half feel guilty, but he bore me no grudges.

Another one of Dennis's bugbears was the girls who worked in the peepshow down in Walker Court.

SEE THOSE NAKED DANCING GIRLS!

Hooked by the yellow sign, you went into what looked like a toilet cubicle (and often smelled like one), stuck 50p in the slot, a letterbox flap creaked open, and you were an instant voyeur. On the other side of the glass two or three naked girls danced for their unseen 'admirers'.

Dancing! No joy was involved. Nor would any sensible person expect there to be. Goosepimples, pubes, trickle of sweat: the punters had a view of every last detail. But all the girls could see was a row of eyes looking through slots: hard eyes, bloodshot eyes, ravishing eyes, disapproving eyes. Strippers have some kind of rapport with their audience, a tenuous link with showbiz they can draw comfort from. Not the peepshow girls. They chew gum and oscillate their arses just enough not to lay themselves open to some trumped-up charge under the Trades Descriptions Act. It would have been juicily ironic, for some punter to report them for not dancing enough. But it was unlikely: the kind of men who used peepshows would never have the guts.

Tacky or not, these girls had the same rights as other workers. Health and Safety laws decreed they had to have a break every hour. Their 'rest room' was just across the hallway from the *Razzle* office. After a steaming shower to wash off the lingering stares they sat and relaxed with a smoke and a cuppa. Their telly was doing Dennis's head in: the amplified yapping of *Neighbours* and *Take the High Road* ruined all attempts at concentration. Dennis would be poring over something and the voice of Mrs Mack would float into the room: 'Och aye, I dinnae ken the young folk today, always off for the high-life in Dundee . . .'

'How can people expect me to paginate a magazine with that soap rubbish going on?'

It didn't bother me. Mrs Mack's fluting grumbles brought a fresh Highland breeze into our oily Soho existence.

I often paused for a chat with the peepshow girls. Despite the work they weren't hard-faced or dumb, just intelligent working-class girls trying to earn a crust. I felt hesitant, but though I worked for a girlie mag they didn't despise me for it. We were all in it together. Their bodies were commodities, but so was my brain. The porno biz had production-line values and cared little for human dignity, spiritual or physical. The girls saved their hatred for the eyes that watched them. They might have respected a man with the guts to admit his interest, but to hide behind a letterbox was pathetic.

So they wanted an eyeful, then? To get revenge the girls would sometimes come right up to the letterbox, filling the punter's entire field of vision with pubes, blotting out his eyeballing rape with a meaningless scribble of crinkled hair.

The basement of 6 Brewer Street housed a porno cinema. Its dusty light bulbs twinkled uselessly in the grey daylight, a desperate attempt to attract an audience. The sad little Italian who manned the paybox was always trying to lure me in. Every time I went past he grinned and made some helpless gesture, muttering about the wind or the rain. What he wanted wasn't custom, just a bit of company. One lunchtime, desperate to get away from the office, but fed up with wandering, I took up his offer and went inside. Just for somewhere to sit.

The steps into the auditorium seemed to have been placed at a demonic angle, threatening to tip the unwary punter headfirst on to the greasy carpet. Up in front of me, magnified, pink and booming, a fat penis sawed its way in and out of a splayed vagina. I doubt if anything would have distracted these spectators, but I wasn't going to walk down the aisle. I found a seat at the back. As my eyes got accustomed to the gloom I saw about a dozen men, pop-eyes glued to the screen. They took care to sit a proper distance from each other, to avoid unwelcome proximity, but also for privacy. The row of seats immediately in front of me had only one occupant and it rocked gently, almost imperceptibly, but with an audible squeak.

'Nick, get a tenner out of petty cash.'
'What for?'
'Nip out and get two pads of Basildon Bond, a nice pale

blue if you can. Forty matching envelopes. Forty stamps – second class. And some perfume.'

'Perfume?'

'Charlie. Paco Rabanne. Something like that?'

'Envelopes? Perfume? What's all this for, Dennis?'

'Why do I always get this backchat every time I ask for anything?' he grumbled, grasping for a cigarette.

I had to admit, the *Razzle* 'Pen Pal' was a novel idea – a busty model who'd send handwritten replies to punters who wrote in to her. It was a written version of the dirty phone call.

A con, of course. The replies were from me. £1 for each letter was Dennis's deal. Two sides of an ordinary Basildon Bond pad was the agreed definition, the only condition being that I had to do it in my spare time, not at the office.

It seemed like an avalanche, but I suppose it was a few dozen letters at most. If all *Razzle*'s readers had responded to the idea I'd have had to write 40,000 replies! (though if I'd kept Dennis to his £1 a go deal I'd have been laughing). My handwriting was crappy, so I had to make it as curvy and as feminine as possible, a misty puff of Charlie adding that convincing touch of girliness. While my friends were at the pub having a laugh, I sat at home getting writer's cramp. Doing lines at school was a laugh by comparison. The writers had all supplied their names and addresses. What were they thinking of, trusting us to that extent? I could have dropped any of them in it, ruined their lives, got them the sack, broken up their marriages. We knew far too much.

The Pen Pals changed each issue. One month I had to be Paula the busty blonde, the next month Sharon the compact brunette. Not too difficult for someone like me, an expert practitioner of porno prose. It soon became obvious that the same punters were writing in every month, so not only did I have to try and change my writing, I had to think of new tacks: if I was a dirty bitch who loved oral last month, this month I had to come on as a shy virgin just waiting to be seduced.

Even two or three letters weren't enough for some of them. They wanted to meet up and sent me the addresses of restaurants and a time to meet them:

I'll be the blond guy in the Armani suit. I need those trendy loose-cut trousers to hide my iron-hard cock when I'm thinking of you . . .

You look like a lady who enjoys fine wines and good food. Do you like prawn cocktail? I'm going to coat my grand penis in Thousand Island Dressing so you can lick it off slowly . . .

They were only half joking. I feared it could easily get out of hand. What if one of them fell in love with me, became obsessed by my red lips and pink nipples? There were thousands of nutters out there – city weirdos, mad yokels, men with bat ears and wiry hair, men driven bonkers by years of loneliness and rejection. One slap in the face too many and they'd freak. What would they do when they found out they'd been conned, that their fragrant dolly bird was really a moustachioed Midlander in an anorak?

One wrote and said he'd wait for me after work. It terrified me. A stalker was out there, waiting for me. At night, when I left, I looked nervously up and down the street. Soho is never empty. Lurking is par for the course. It could be anyone. But there was a man in an Esso baseball cap who kept looking across at our doorway. That was him, I was convinced of it.

Then I remembered. Fool! He'd be looking for a woman. I could leave in safety. Legging it to the 159 bus stop, I couldn't help feeling sorry for the poor sap on his hopeless mission.

Part-owner of our litho house, Raj popped into the office on the flimsiest excuse, always in the hope of catching us halfway through an orgy or something. Finding us hard at work over our typewriters his disappointment was obvious. Convinced that we'd become expert in covering up, he hovered expectantly. 'This Miss Dolly Bird,' he'd say, sliding a brown finger indecently across her nakedness. 'You must get me an introduction.'

'Sorry, no can do. Professional ethics. We're not running an escort agency, Raj.'

He looked hurt at the suggestion. 'No hanky-panky! I am an educated man. I can introduce her to the best things. Good food. Fine wine. Theatrical entertainments.'

'And a good intercontinental shag.'

'Please!'

'No, she wouldn't be interested.'

'Not interested in meeting a sophisticated gentleman?' Raj fixed me with a jealous glare. 'Ha! Because you have already corrupted her, seduced her with your trickery, destroyed her spirit with your love-them-and-leave-them, Jack-the-lad philosophy.'

'I've never touched her. I don't even know her.'

'Pah! Even now she is crying into her duvet over the way you have treated her. You think your posh job gives you *carte blanche* with susceptible women.'

Raj had been pestering us to get him involved in a photo session, convinced that when the lens caps were snapped back on and the films put away in their little canisters, the models rewarded everyone for their hard work with sexual favours.

And for that reason we could never have him at a proper photo session in a studio. Instead we invited him down to Bottom Row.

Bottom Row was a street full of stereotypes: willing housewives, drippy husbands, randy plumbers, frustrated mothers-in-law. Living clichés brought to life in a monthly photo-story which spoofed those romance mags for teenage girls.

It could have been any street in Britain. In reality, more often than not, the kitchen or bedroom scenes were done at Jim Stone's terraced house in Hackney. Nosy neighbours must have been intrigued by all the comings and goings, girls with make-up boxes and leather minis. If they'd peeped through the windows they'd have been outraged: naked girls sitting round drinking Nescafé and grumbling about periods and pimples.

I'd written a script especially for Raj. A couple were off for a wedding-anniversary lunch at the local tandoori. Raj was to play the randy waiter. Dennis asked me to take the part of the loving husband. I refused. In an act of charity, I managed to get a grudging £25 fee for an out-of-work drinking pal from the Belsize Tavern. Jim had persuaded the owner of his local greasy spoon to lend us his premises in return for a few photos to perk up his walls. After the midday rush the place was tarted up with a few Taj Mahal pictures and a pottery elephant and, hey presto!, Pete's café became the Golden Duck of Bombay.

Now Raj had got his wish he was getting cold feet. He entered nervously with his briefcase, which was quickly snatched from his hands and replaced by a teatowel and a fake menu. When the woman finally got her kit off, Raj's tongue wobbled like a water bed and his eyes reddened, as if someone had spoon-fed him a tin of chilli powder. When it came to it he was as shy as hell. He was learning the lesson we'd all learned. Eroticism was all in the punter's mind: faced with the perspiring and perfumed reality men didn't know which way to look.

Like the *Fiesta* Flasher episode, this one also had a twist. After sex, Raj's favourite topic was cricket. He knew his stuff and had a job as cricket correspondent for an Indian newspaper. When the Indian cricket team came over that summer Raj was invited to their farewell luncheon – only to find himself the target of some sniggering. He demanded to know what the joke was. Out came a copy of *Razzle*, with Raj's face grinning out from between the boobs of a large naked lady.

*   *   *

Around the middle of May I went AWOL. I intended to go back, but the two days I'd planned soon stretched into a week. A fatal break. In Belsize Park the girls were putting on their summer dresses and sandals, tripping up to the launderette and the mini-market in shorts and sleeveless blouses. I was as easily worked up as a Victorian – a pretty ankle, a slender neck, bottoms in indigo Wrangler's, the hazy outline of a bra strap through white – all those things thrilled me. But more: they reminded me what I'd been missing. I'd filled my brain with so much porno crap I'd lost sight of real femininity.

I had to jack it in, and now, before any permanent damage was done to my personality.

I felt like I'd betrayed all these girls, by making out that their beauty could be bought for the price of a *Razzle*. Sex was great, of course it was, and women were fabulous, naked or dressed. But girlie mags could never capture that magic, it was as elusive as vaporized perfume.

There was no way I was going to have the shackles put back on, nor go through the humiliating process of thinking up naff excuses. I'd used them all before anyway: food poisoning, sickness and diarrhoea, colds, flu, even measles. I didn't have the guts to formally resign, the thought of Dennis's disappointment filled me with horror. I just never went in again.

7 Soho Stories: Part One

After another three months dossing on the doorstep I got myself a new job. One worth boasting about this time. Compared with the ethical half-world of girlie mags, advertising was deliciously legit, as clean and wholesome as a Daz commercial. No excuses necessary. In fact, the only problem was persuading people of my lowly status. No, I didn't do that Crunchie ad on telly. No, I'd never coined any jingles that kids hummed in the schoolyard. But I bought *Campaign* every week, spoke ad-speak ('I see KLM are in for a three-way pitch with BBDO, DBB and RCWS . . .') and kidded myself I belonged to a world of wit, wine bars and Filofaxes.

Working conditions were seductive: a pine desk, a swivelly chair and – bliss! – an electric typewriter with interchangeable daisy wheels. Writing in italics made bugger-all difference to the dullness of my Pontin's Holidays copy, but it looked good. Style and protocol were everything here. Our brainstorming sessions were held in a boardroom with a giant polished table and secretaries were bidden to bring us tea, coffee and fruit juice. After the slapdash come-as-you-please of *Razzle* it was great to be treated importantly.

I had money to burn. That Christmas, in a last-ditch attempt to win back Elaine, I strutted into Dixons in Queensway and slapped down £200 for a Pentax camera. Disgusted by my extravagance, she sent it back with a terse note saying in terms not to waste my money on her like this. It would not change anything between us. The sooner

I accepted that, the sooner I would find happiness by rebuilding my life. It was signed 'Love, Elaine'.

Love! Why did women write 'love' when they obviously didn't mean it? Maybe that's what those powwows in the schoolyard were all about: impromptu advice sessions where girls swapped ideas for cruel jokes and perfected their piss-taking techniques. Writing 'love' fooled the victim into thinking there'd been a Freudian slip. Yes! he'd think, she does still love me. And the poor sap would scan the letter over and over, word by word, looking for anything that could be twisted into, 'I want to say sorry, I'm just making you wait.'

In my heart of hearts I knew Elaine's letter might just as well have started 'Dear Sir' and ended 'Yours faithfully'. Money couldn't buy me love. Lennon and McCartney had taught me that. Nor could it buy me a second chance. Just a second camera I didn't need. (As a penance, I should have gone out in the streets wearing both of them, so everyone could see what a fool I was: Nick 'Two Cameras' Whittaker.)

Back at the agency I struggled with the Pontin's copy. ('No witty stuff,' they warned. 'We want holiday feelgood and value for money.') Devoid of inspiration, I watched the girls in the office across the street. When one of them caught me out and waved, I quickly looked away. Too long in the girlie biz had made guilt an automatic reflex. But the next time she waved I could see it wasn't a piss-take. By a complex series of mime and hand signals we arranged to meet up for a lunchtime drink.

Waiting on the corner, I started to get the wind up. I didn't even dare light a ciggie: what if she hated smokers? Separated by windows and a veil of taxi fumes, our flirtation had always been a bit unreal. What was she like close up? What if she had spots? A hare lip? A glass eye? What if she had a Brummie accent and was as thick as shit?

Fortunately Claire had none of these defects. As soon as she skipped out into the street I breathed in the smell of jasmine soap and London cleverness and couldn't believe my luck.

Our hour at Piers, the local wine bar, turned out to be a chatty success. According to dating lore, making a girl laugh is a good start. A pity it wasn't intentional. If anyone had reason to fear the other's thickness Claire had. I'd always assumed 'Piers' was part of some seaside theme, not merely the owner's name. In the Midlands people just didn't have names like Piers.

Soon we had a regular thing going. The January frost didn't matter. We eschewed the warmth (and expense) of Piers and walked hand in hand around Hyde Park. The ducks loved us, pattering around our feet as we tossed them bread and talked about books, films and travel. I kept shtum about my time at *Razzle*. Even the name, so puerile and sleazy, disgusted me. Advertising was my world now. And Claire – clean, bobbed, well-spoken – was the kind of handmaiden who went with the territory.

Just one problem: what about Connie? Since our first date we'd been seeing each other on and off for a few months. I didn't have the guts to ditch her. Why should I? She'd done nothing wrong. She obviously adored me, showering me with tapes and books and shirts, all accompanied by romantic memos on pink notepaper. I was the best thing that had ever happened to her, she said.

But I'd got the taste for co-habiting. Having a girlfriend who still lived at home seemed like a step backwards. Connie could only come out two or three times a week and often baulked at staying the night since it meant a row with her mum and dad.

One evening, after popcorn and sticky hand-holding at the Westbourne Grove Odeon, I went back to Claire's flat-share. On a promise, I thought. But kissing was as far as we went. Claire apologized, but she believed we weren't committed enough. I pretended to respect that, but I was furious. I spent the rest of the night being a pig, grunting, shrugging, feigning indifference. It was all too much. Even the moths were having sex, frolicking on the inside of the lampshade, wings flittering in orgasmic delight.

Next morning, Claire woke me with a cup of tea. As she knelt down by the bed, her carelessly buttoned shirt showing her breasts, I thought maybe she'd relented. Last night had just been a test: after I'd swigged the tea she'd jump in for an early morning cuddle.

But the only triangle I was going to get near was a brittle triangle of wholemeal toast meanly smeared with marmalade.

Things cooled off soon after. And not just because of the sexual embargo. Claire confessed she already had a steady boyfriend – and one of her flatmates had blabbed about me staying the night. I wasn't bothered. At least not until I saw him one day, staring across at me from Claire's office. He was a tough-looking bastard, one of those public-school rugby-playing types with muscles, blue eyes and a jaw you could use as a set square. How could I compete? In any case, why had she wanted me when she had a hunk like that? I refused to face up to the notion that I might have been her piece of rough.

A few weeks later, advertising gave me the big E too. It seemed I didn't quite fit in with the image they wanted to project. Worse, I was too bolshy to make the effort. What? I have to wear red braces and a dicky bow to write fucking Pontin's adverts? Being clever simply wasn't enough: you had to look clever as well. I didn't mind writing crap about glorious yellow sands and fun-filled family days, but I was damned if I'd make myself into a show-dummy to do it.

I could have gone on longer, but they were beginning to get suspicious. We had a pitch for some sham-glamorous face-powder that claimed to make women glittery and exciting and beautiful, but all I could think of was girls called Sharon and Tracey in Wakefield and Lewisham dusting it on and trying to find happiness with a bloke who just wanted a shag. To me it was all bollocks. Albeit high-class, well-rewarded and sophisticated bollocks. I thought I'd escaped for a moment, but I'd gone from covering up for men to being a barrow boy.

We sat in the boardroom on leather armchairs and racked our brains for ideas. I was imploding with boredom, counting specks of dust in the sunlight. Bloated faces lurched at me. 'Got any ideas, Nick?' I shrugged and grinned. But they wanted great slogans. Dumb insolence is the term they use. I sat and hoped beyond hope that I'd get away with it. Secretly I just wanted the end to come.

A succession of temping jobs and further spells on the dole followed, some of them in Soho. I dreaded bumping into Dennis. Instead, popping out for a sandwich one day, I met Colin – now working with Dennis at Paul Raymond.

In the two years since I'd gone AWOL from *Razzle* there'd been big changes. Dennis had added *Club* to his portfolio and brought production from Archer Street to Brewer Street, assuming the title of managing editor of the pair, and leaving Nevile Player in charge of *Men Only* and *Escort*. Colin had never been happy with running *Fiesta*, even less so when it meant upping sticks for exile in Essex. When Dennis approached him, he was more than pleased to move back to a job in London, despite all their previous rumbles. From what Colin said, Dennis might be prepared to forgive me. Since he'd started empire building, Dennis needed more staff: a production editor for the two titles. He reckoned I'd fit the bill perfectly.

The damp building I'd done a runner from was now warm and dry and full of life. The kebab man had long been banished. So had the peepshow girls, their rest room now converted into a new office for the growing editorial staff.

Girlie mags had never featured on my reading list, but I'd been unable to resist one peep in a newsagent's – just to see who'd stepped into my shoes at *Razzle*. The name – female and exotically foreign – intrigued me. Despite myself I couldn't help a twinge of jealousy. Could she be as good as I'd been? Now I had chance to meet her. A well-spoken Londoner with trendy specs and a penchant for black, Maria was the kind of girl I imagined on the fashion desk of *Cosmopolitan* or *Harpers*. Names mattered to her: the right names to wear, the right shops for kitchen equipment, the right places for a night out.

I don't know how she'd ended up on *Razzle*. Like me, I expect she'd just been looking for an opening into journalism and taken the first chance that came. Whatever, she'd quickly grasped the rules. Fuck this, fanny that, spunk, prick and tit – the words clattered off her typewriter with secretarial efficiency. When it came to it, women knew as many dirty words as we men did. But she was only following a formula. It was off-the-peg pornography, a simple technique of stringing certain words together in a certain order.

I'd felt bad enough, but it must have been even harder for a woman to write that filth. No, Maria reasoned, it was only fantasy. She was quite able to distance herself from it. It wasn't her who was being had over the bonnet of a Jaguar or sucking off some shithead builder.

Like prostitutes, we'd learned the technique of faking orgasm, of making it look real. As the keys clippety-clopped against the paper, the real Maria was elsewhere, mentally shopping in Harvey Nichols, matching wallpapers and curtains for her new flat in Holborn, checking out Delia Smith recipes.

Until the eighties girlie mags had been men-only affairs. Women did the stripping and made the editor's tea, but men remained at the helm. Women were the *raison d'être*, yet they had little part in the production. Things were changing. *Razzle, Escort* and *Men Only* all had female editorial staff, decent girls with IQs and middle-class values – yet they didn't mind at all objectifying their sisters for the pleasure of the nation's wankers.

Over at *Penthouse* and *Forum* women already had the top jobs. Had they been feminists they'd have been in an excellent position for sabotage. Yet none of them saw girlie-mag readers as a threat, just sad loners without a real-life woman of their own. Wasn't it better for them to spill some seed over a glossy mag than go out and commit a rape?

Ironically, I was the one who got so indignant while they handled it well, with businesslike efficiency, career-driven energy and, when necessary, disdain that was royal and icy. These girls didn't need pseudo-gents like me to protect them.

In the foreseeable future even Paul Raymond Publications would have a woman at the top. Primogeniture hadn't gone to plan. Howard Raymond, a quiet and decent young man, turned out not to be interested in his father's legacy. Dad didn't seem to mind being labelled a porn baron, but for someone more sensitive it would be torture. But this was the eighties. Women were only too willing to step into the breach. Howard's sister, Debbie, had given up showbusiness and wanted to learn the titillation trade. Paul Raymond was a doting dad, but to avoid charges of nepotism he apprenticed her to Nevile. She was going to have to start at the bottom like everyone else, churning out confessions and blurbs, marking up copy for the typesetters.

While I got upset and prim about men not respecting women, tough gals like Debbie just saw a mass market of wankers worth exploiting. Why should they care about revenge or feminist dialectic when, somewhere out there, was a parallel nation, a country full of men with secret sex lives who would fund their Porsches and pay the mortgage on their West End flats?

Dennis resented us fraternizing with the Archer Street folk. All the more so when it involved cackling and having a drag with Debbie: she'd be tomorrow's boss. We were making connections that figured in his nightmares: a conspiracy of minions and anarchic bosses. We were all young. We liked Dire Straits and Queen. Debbie liked a laugh. Although paid a nominal salary, she had a fat bank account and important contacts. Paul Raymond was landlord to half the bars and clubs in Soho, so a night out with Debbie was usually a round of drinks on a tab that was more often than not waived by a club manager who wanted to stay sweet with Raymond.

Dennis's number one *bête noire* was Nevile, the laid-back editor of *Escort* and *Men Only*. Laconic, chummy, scruffily stylish, he was everything Dennis wasn't. Worse, *Escort* was riding high and Nevile didn't even seem to be trying. Whenever any of us dropped by, there were no feverishly clacking typewriters, no raised voices. Just Nevile with his feet up and a smouldering ciggie in the ashtray. Yet *Escort* appeared on time and did well. He arranged outrageous photo shoots and always got away with it. When Paul Raymond banned Readers' Wives for aesthetic reasons Dennis caved in but Nevile carried on regardless. He got away with it because Raymond knew damn well he'd got a top editor and he'd never find anyone better tuned in with the masturbatory zeitgeist.

But at least Dennis had managed to get his secretary at last, as befitted his managing editor status. Yvonne answered his phone, made his tea, kept his files in order. And more. Yvonne did what so many men wished their secretaries did: she stripped off too. As a jobbing model she'd never make the big-time, but she'd pick up modest cheques as long as her figure and face lasted. Hers wasn't one of those names that become part of the tit-fancier's *Who's Who* – Samantha Fox, Linda Lusardi, Maria Whittaker – names that become part of the common lingo. But to readers of *Club* and *Razzle*, she was a familiar face. She'd appeared in one of those 'educational' videos for married couples. She'd even, so rumour had it, done a couple of hard-core films: no pissing or donkeys or anything sick – just her and her boyfriend having a shag and getting paid a useful hundred quid apiece for it.

She was in a curious position: everyone in the *Razzle* offices had seen her naked, and her boyfriend knew that we'd all seen her naked too. But, so what, it was all in a day's work. Diplomatic silence was the norm, though occasionally we couldn't help speculating on their sex lives.

The arrangement was uneasily symbiotic. Not only did Yvonne appear in the magazines as well as being Dennis's secretary, but her boyfriend was a photographer and depended on Dennis for work. Yvonne, in turn, put up with a hell of a lot of shit. But she scored points whenever she could. One evening Dennis demanded tea five minutes before hometime. There were no teabags left and Yvonne was damned if she'd go out to the shop for some. Instead she retrieved a used one from the bin and squeezed an extra cup's worth of juice out of it. Dennis slurped it down without comment.

After the posey bullshit of advertising, returning to *Razzle* was like putting on a comfy pair of slippers. We were already outsiders, so why bother trying to impress? Sharp suits and jazzy ties would never change anyone's prejudices. We could have worn slippers too, no one would have cared. Nor did our workplace have to be a status trip for the boss. Other people's offices looked luxurious, but it was deceptive, just a corporate ego trip that enveloped them with gimmickry: static nylon carpets, double-glazing, lifts to wait for, security guards, passes. Paul Raymond offered none of that. But in place of the luxuries came an enviable freedom. I could lean at the window, smell the strawberries, harken to the barrow boys. Best of all though, was those hours of amusement provided by the punters.

Soho's reputation refuses to die. It remains a place of pilgrimage. Remote and mythical, it exerts an irresistible power. Stories are legion: what you can buy, what you can do, how much fun you can have. There's a desperation to believe. Throughout the year, rain or shine, a rag-taggle bunch comes looking for thrills. Japanese tourists, rowdy football fans and lonely businessmen throng through Walker Court, a narrow passage choked with kebab fumes and exhaust. Darting glances to each side they flail through the rustling strip curtains.

Soho's straight traders often bemoan the area's reputation, but on many days you couldn't help thinking they were all in it together, the porn agenda forced on them all by association. It wasn't just the fruit barrows, like organic marital-aids shops, laid out with provocative bananas and luscious green-nippled melons, but the fashion stalls too, decked with dangling bras, silky knickers and buttoned minis. Even the butcher's, its window full of skinned rabbits resembling giant pricks, offered unsettling hints of sex and mortality.

The owners of Lovejoy's bookshop probably thought they'd hit on the perfect name. Those advertising bods would have thought it exquisitely witty. But it'd be hard to think of anything more miserably inappropriate. Sadwank's or Looksly's maybe. For my own attempt at wit, I'd suggest Abasement, since the Adult Section is invariably downstairs and out of sight, pervaded by the distinctive smell of loneliness, a joyless mixture of anonymous perfume and KY jelly. Browsers are presided over by a man at a high counter. To relieve the tedium he usually has a crony with him. Between them they've seen it all, every wanking archetype. Each customer is processed with unsmiling eyes, relieved of his cash and categorized with an exchange of looks:

'Hen-pecked hubby with a secret yen for young blond guys.'

'Skinny four-eyes who wants to bury his face in between a pair of 44DDs.'

'Management type who wants to have his arse spanked by a tart in a gymslip.'

Soho today isn't half what it's cracked up to be. Years of legislation and council by-laws have cut off its balls. Compared with Amsterdam or Hamburg it's a rip-off. Despised by the law and by public opinion, as far as officialdom goes, if anyone gets fleeced it serves them right for being perverts. Gloomy clip-joints continue to thrive, luring punters inside with promises of non-stop porno action.

It still puzzles me: why on earth, knowing as much as I did, did I let Connie persuade me it'd be fun to visit one together?

She'd reached a particular point in the relationship: the sex mad phase. A fortnight previously, returning from a weekend in Paris, I'd taken her to see a porno film across from the Gare du Nord while we were waiting for the train. She'd picked up some funny ideas. All the way back to Boulogne she lay back in her seat, stretching her legs across the compartment and rubbing her stockinged toes against my crotch. The nodal points just under my ears glowed red with embarrassment. Connie giggled like mad. She thought it was a hot adventure.

If anyone knew about the threats and rip-offs endemic in clip-joints, I should. I would have known damn well there were no uncut Swedish porno films on show. As for Continental hostesses . . . humbug! We paid the token £2 to the crone on the door and went down the dimly lit stairs. The furnishings of the 'exotic club surroundings' were as glamorous as a lorry drivers' caff: tubular steel chairs and greasy tablecloths. No one else was in there. A projector showed blurred slides, one at a time, women in bikinis, so tame they might have been snapped on Mablethorpe beach.

The drinks menu arrived. If this woman was a Continental hostess then the continent must have been Antarctica and she came from a family of polar bears. Connie and I exchanged nervous glances. For politeness' sake I chose a couple of Cokes. The bill followed closely: £46.00. £23 for each flat and warm glassful.

'I think you've made a mistake,' I said. 'I'm not paying this.'

Couldn't I see that I was walking straight into the trap? A heavy suddenly blocked what little light there was from the doorway. Big trouble. I only had £15 on me. While I was held hostage Connie had to run round to the cash machine at Piccadilly Circus. All kind of things ran through my mind. Was I in credit? What if the machine had the NOT IN SERVICE flag up? What if Connie did a runner? Down here, no one would hear me even if I yelled for help. I could be killed and buried in a backyard so tiny no one even knew it existed. No one would ever find me.

After an anxious twenty minutes she returned with the money and we fled.

Not long after I arrived back at *Razzle*, Paul Raymond gave the go-ahead for the magazine to become a full-sized hundred-page monthly. To trumpet the occasion a launch party was held at the Café Royale.

Lured by the promise of meeting models in the flesh, the wholesalers and sales guys flocked. Since it was happening on the QT, no one would see them if they got kissed by a model or two. They had pretty wives and lovely kids, they had good jobs and neat semis in the suburbs – yet it wasn't enough. They still felt they'd missed out by not capturing a trophy wife – a blonde with luscious lipsticked lips, one who dressed in fishnet tights and leather minis. They thought that was the pinnacle of male achievement.

All men, suits or brickies, are the same underneath: hairy, primitive and lustful. At least Tone and Phil had the guts to be honest: they liked tit and they didn't care who knew it. These men in suits were too scared: having adopted the disguise they became doubly scared of being open about their fancies. Their wives, employers, public opinion . . . they all expected them to be different men.

Imagining it would be a posh do, I'd gone and bought myself an off-the-peg suit from Burtons. An hour into the party I was beginning to wish I hadn't bothered. Middle-class, middle-aged, middle-management, the guests here were no better than the baying crowd I'd fought my way out of at the strip show fifteen years earlier. I'd always hated the suit as a sign of conformity; tonight I hated it doubly so, for the way it conferred a false dignity on us, highlighted the double standards. The strip show had been bad enough, but we were just lads then. Here the imbalance between the half-naked girls and the smirking men in suits seemed doubly obscene.

So many men are able to use their social roles to deflect suspicion: as if headmasters, shop managers and airline pilots are smoothly asexual. Is it blasphemy to suggest that financiers wank? Or that chairmen of privatized water companies dress up in suspenders? They're all men underneath. Why are we so surprised by scandals involving businessmen and politicians? Maybe we aren't. Maybe it's actually comforting to know that those snooty besuited highflyers are, at the end of the day, as much slaves to their balls as the sweatiest hod-carrier.

Compared to Kilburn, the West End offered all kinds of diversions. Sometimes we went to Pizzaland in Shaftesbury Avenue. The young-at-hearts in the art room were all mad about Chinese food: you could get a decent fill for about £3 at some of the little places in Chinatown. I wasn't that keen, but I sometimes got one of them to bring me back a foil tin of Singapore Noodles.

One lunchtime Colin and I ambled off to the Hayward gallery to see an exhibition of surrealism. We didn't get back till nearly three. Dennis was furious. It was bad enough the art room lingering over a table of steaming Dim Sum, but to neglect work for a bloody art exhibition!

That was our trouble: Colin and I, all of us really. We were too bloody arty-farty to be wasting our lives creating porn for the country's wanktocracy.

Though I was no longer on the editorial staff, I didn't mind doing freelance stuff for extra money. One regular spot was the 'Saucy Sexword' in *Razzle*.

It appealed to the schoolboy in our readers. Despite the subject matter I was enormously proud of the cryptics and anagrams:

1) Bare Ann pats Di perhaps if she takes these off (3,3,7)

3) Thingie to put on at bedtime! (7)

5) TUC sperm could be a tasty teatime treat! (7)

7) Backward bog people might use it for oral sex (3)

9) Vi grins maybe because she's no longer one of them (7)

11) Stud fucked ten – and he's still a learner! (7)

I prided myself on doing a professional job. It was as good as the *Times* crossword, perfectly symmetrical 15 X 15, except all the answers were dirty.

Alongside the crossword was a wordsearch called the 'Dirty Dozen' and one in which the punter was required to change a word, DATE to SHAG in four moves. Such intellectual effort; I really was wasted in pornography.

As well as its puzzle page, *Razzle* also had a literary column. Colin had wangled several publishers into sending him review copies. Each parcel, delivered by bike at Paul Raymond's expense, brought on bibliophilistic raptures. Box on desk, parcel tape cast aside in writhing loops, Colin lifted out the books, breathed in their shiny newness and felt their weight, smiling the kind of smile men have when cradling their lover's breasts. Dennis watched these ceremonies with ill-disguised annoyance.

'What's in it for the readers, Colin?'

A good question. Few of them were likely to rush out for the latest Gabriel García Márquez or a biography of Stanley Baldwin. Occasionally they might be hooked by some sexy extract, but cough up £13.99 for a hardback? Not likely! There was precious little in it for the publishers come to that. It kept Colin happy, though.

Not all the books were highbrow. Dennis wouldn't have

stood for such lordly indifference to the punters. We included the usual sex manuals, like *The Joy of Sex*, with its sketches of couples making love. It was a perennial best-seller, now in its nth edition. The naked couple, sketched in brown pencil, seemed to have been with us for years, the woman with her pageboy haircut, her bearded lover, an Open University lecturer two-timing his wife. Since the antics of this pair were only mildly titillating, the book's appeal centred on the advice and encouragement it offered to its many readers. Using the word 'joy' in the title was marketing genius, a word so rarely applied in British culture until then.

What lent this naked pair a certain credibility was the fact that they were so un-British. Even stark naked, they were unspecifically, but unmistakably, European: French, Danish, or most likely German. Readers would have been sceptical about a British couple teaching them about sex. But the French knew how to kiss, the Germans and the Danes made great porn films, the Dutch made great love after a deep toke of cannabis.

Nevertheless, the book's success baffled me. Was it really possible that so many men needed advice on how to find a woman's clitoris, how to suck a nipple, how to bring about shattering climaxes? Men had a touching belief in manuals, as if success was based on a correct application of mechanical theory. At least they were trying. They knew modern women wanted an orgasm and they did their best to deliver. Thirty years previously no man would have given it a second thought.

Mac, *Club*'s assistant editor, was a sandy-haired Scot who'd previously worked on a motorbike mag. He lived the part, arriving each morning in a squeaking set of leathers, a jovial Gregor Samsa unzipping and pop-studding himself to find that – whew! – there was still a human being inside.

Like recruits to the foreign legion, porno people were always vague about their past, hinting at secrets and mistakes they were running from: they'd usually been misunderstood or sacked by morons for standing up for their principles. But they always brought their obsessions with them. Before long, Mac had persuaded Dennis to instigate a *Club* motorbike page. They'd use the shiny bikes as seduction accessories, photographing them with naked women all over the place. It wasn't quite what Mac had had in mind. It was a perversion, a distraction from the true mechanical beauty of the machines. But heck, it meant Mac would get to test-drive some beauties.

We got on OK for a while, Mac and I. He admired me for having worked in advertising. The turning point came when I told Mac I'd written a short tourist guide to Edinburgh. He was impressed, until I told him I'd only ever been there once, on a trainspotting trip back in 1973. From then on he refused to take me seriously.

I was a lousy production editor, far too laid-back to enforce the discipline necessary to make things run like clockwork. That things ran to schedule was as much due to the diligence of Colin and Mac and the art-room lads as to any effort on my part. Colin said I was so laid-back I ought to put in a requisition for a sofa-bed.

Dennis wouldn't have laughed. I had to look like I was at least trying. To this end I kept two giant ledgers, one each for *Club* and *Razzle*, with columns detailing the dates when copy was sent to the typesetter's, when proofs were due back, when corrected proofs were to be returned, when galleys had to be pasted up with artwork and dispatched to the repro house, when proofs were expected, when ozalids were expected. I was a go-between, endlessly on the phone to typesetter's, repro house and printer's, alternatively complaining and apologizing. Dennis heard me doing the latter one day and insisted I be more stern: we were their customers, we paid their wages, we didn't have to grovel to them!

A computer virgin, I naïvely believed that buying one

would help me no end. Dennis remained sceptical, but I pointed out that we were in the second half of the eighties and ought to be facing the future. A computer would streamline production. A week later the PC arrived, an Amstrad with a forbidding stack of manuals. We unboxed it, set up all the wires. I turned to find half a dozen faces staring at me, much as a community of cave-dwellers might have looked at the first wheel salesman.

'How exactly will it help us?' asked Dennis.

I switched it on. We looked at the C:> prompt and the winking cursor. What next? I flicked through a manual, desperately seeking a section headed 'Girlie Magazines: streamlining of production' – but it was an absurd optimism. I didn't even know what software was. Eager faces turned stern. People began to drift away, moaning about my stupidity, my laughable pretensions to be at the cutting edge. Dennis gave me one of his disappointed looks.

'Make sure you put the dust cover on,' he said sternly. He knew that computers hated dust.

I put the cover on. It never came off again. The one good thing was that no one from Archer Street ever came to see this £800 white elephant 'in action'.

The technical imperatives of porn bored me to tears. Punters were happy enough with tits and a fanny to look at – did they really care about the flesh tones being 100 per cent authentic? If, as Dennis insisted, punters wanted the printing to be so good they could see the goosebumps, the soft down and the auburn highlights on each pubic hair, what about those men who wanked in black and white? And those ancient Romans whose only porno thrill was a naked discus thrower on the side of a vase? Surely sexual excitement was a cerebral thing as much as visual?

To Dennis, such ideas were heresy. Determined to make sure I played the part (even if he was pulling the strings) he sent me on a mission to the printer's. Unless we put our foot down occasionally they'd try getting away with murder.

'Don't take any bullshit,' he warned. 'As my production editor you have full right to make demands.'

Oh joy! Two days on a godforsaken windswept industrial estate in Tyne and Wear.

The subject matter of my trip contrasted curiously with the business privileges. I stayed in a posh hotel in Durham and had meals on expenses. But I was totally fed up. If only I'd been driven, a young man determined to prove himself, scrabble up the ambition ladder. If only I could have got excited, angry, demanding about the density of dots on Lola's tits. Shouldn't it be 2 per cent more on the magenta; ease back on the yellow by 4 per cent? Tedious technical bollocks. I yawned my way through the day and was so desperate to get it over with I nodded my assent to anything the management showed me. I didn't give a toss. I was seething. It all took so long, so long that instead of escaping on the last 125 to King's Cross, I had to stay a second night.

Dave, the big boss's deputy, took me out for a curry. But it was more in the line of duty than genuine hospitality. We chatted in a polite blokeish way. He was exactly the young ambitious type I could never be. He could actually get excited about ink densities and grades of paper. And the paper mills of Finland were apparently a must-see some day. Yet I don't think he knew how excited he looked. He envied me, thought I had it made, working with models, looking at sex eight hours a day. But how I envied him, that night anyhow: at least he was going home to a young wife in a frilly nightie. When she took it off she'd be really naked underneath. How the hell could anyone be envious of those who worked in porn?

After our chicken madras and three pints of lager, Dave drove me back to the hotel. As I staggered across the gravel driveway to the door I realized it was the wrong hotel. Arms flailing I rushed across the car park and just managed to stop him before he sped off into the darkness!

*   *   *

Connie and I were taking a week's holiday bumming around on French railways with a rover ticket. Halfway between Marseilles and Bordeaux our train paused at a little station in the Languedoc. Connie had her nose buried in a phrase book, but I saw the station name: Agde. Something clicked. Agde was the home of the world's biggest naturist holiday centre. I'd seen the name loads of times while browsing through *Health & Efficiency*. Before she knew what had hit her, Connie was standing on the platform, phrase book still in hand, looking up the French for 'Excuse me, is that my train disappearing into the distance?'

'What the hell have we got off here for?'

I bought her a *café crème* and tried to explain, but I was digging myself in deeper. She thought she'd gone adventuring with a new bloke – hadn't we sat up till three, smoking Gauloises, swigging Chablis and talking about everything from Dickens to U2? – but the dream was shattered. He was as desperate to ogle as the rest of them. While she flicked through the Thomas Cook timetable looking for the next train, I did my best to persuade her that we needed some ozone.

'Yeah, and I know what O-zone you're after,' she sneered, shoving Thomas Cook back into her rucksack. It was a scorching day in the middle of nowhere. The next train from Agde wasn't for three hours . . .

I appealed to her sense of adventure. Like me she hated the stuffy and inhibited British way of life. Here was a chance to go Continental.

A rickety bus took us out to the holiday centre. Half an hour later we were both starkers on the beach, along with a thousand or so other people. It didn't take any getting used to. Connie was beginning to enjoy herself. She'd only ever seen a couple of penises, now she was surrounded by them: short 'n' fat, long 'n' thin, long 'n' fat, short 'n' wrinkled, roundheads and cavaliers. Some swung past only inches from her face. Between giggles she managed to get out something about a parade of circus elephants.

If we'd been German or French or Danish there'd never have been any argument on the platform. Those Europeans get 'em off at the drop of a hat: first glint of sunshine and the jockeys and bras get flung. Go for a walk in a Copenhagen park in summer and the place is full of nudity and no one bats an eyelid. Not us English, though. Admittedly there's always been nudists, gathering like a wacky cult in little 'sun clubs' behind seven-foot laurel hedges. They play volleyball while the kids from the local comprehensive spy through Dad's birdspotting binoculars. We mock them mercilessly one minute and scrutinize their motives cynically the next.

'Not right, is it, Phyllis? Vicars playing ping-pong with girls, not when they're just, you know, getting to be women and that . . .'

The squeaky rotating postcard stands at Ramsgate and Blackpool are chock-a-block with naturist jokes. Everyone thinks it's one long orgy. How can people possibly be naked together without IT happening? But, here in France, it was all so ordinary. All across the world men were spending millions of pounds a day on girlie mags for the privilege of seeing a naked female. Here, subject to massive overkill, it was nice to look at but no more raunchy or dangerous than a diagram in a biology textbook.

When Maria eventually left for better things Dennis asked me if I wanted to take over the deputy editorship again. I turned his offer down. Aside from the occasional trip to the sticks, production editor was a cushy number. I didn't mind helping out with the odd blurb now and then, but I never wanted to go back to churning out the stuff full-time.

Dennis hated having to advertise. It seemed like every nutter and has-been grabbed the Monday *Guardian* in the hope of finding the doorway to glory: the hopeless and the desperate; the cocky twenty-year-olds who could barely spell; old hands from the nationals who were obviously nearing unwanted retirement. Finding someone who was neither depraved or stupid or over-sensitive was impossible. There was always one who sounded just right – up until the interview anyway. After five minutes of cross-purpose questioning, it turned out they thought *Razzle* was a fashion magazine and ran from the building in horror.

'Bloody waste of time,' Dennis would grumble through a cloud of Dunhill smoke.

He finally took a risk with a green but amiable Ozzie by the name of Les. His first efforts weren't promising. Set the task of producing some confessions, Les presented Dennis with six pages of neatly typed copy that would have gone down a treat at Mills & Boon: lots of women in starched blouses, with slender necks and rosy complexions. A stiff nipple was about as raunchy as it got.

'I thought those Australians were coarse bastards,' Dennis muttered.

Colin and I took Les to one side. We'd all been there. Few people entered the business fully prepared for what they had to do. A whole load of inhibitions had to be shed. We all had to be blooded – spunked maybe.

After our pep-talk Les lurched wildly in the opposite direction:

Pete arched his muscular back as the housewife's mouth slid away from his glistening rod.
'You fucking glorious bitch,' he grunted, shoot-
ing wads of creamy cum into her pleasure-
contorted face . . .

How easy it was, after all. Take away the restraints and the inhibitions and anyone, male or female, could do it.

I suppose you could call it poetic justice. Connie told me she was having an affair with a guy called Tom at her workplace. The news took me aback, but how could I complain? Go for it, I encouraged, desperate to show how unhypocritical I was. Why shouldn't she have a bit on the side? I treated it as a bit of a joke.

We went on a cycling weekend in the Cotswolds and when she had to stop at every phone box to ring and check if he still fancied her, I stood there patiently holding her bike, even looking in my pocket for one more 10p piece when the pips sent her into a panic.

I refused to take it seriously.

But Connie did. For men it's usually just a fuck. Women fall in a big way. I certainly wasn't prepared for her to come and tell me how wonderful it was, how much she was enjoying it.

He'd seduced Connie with novelty. I was determined to expose him and his sleazy *modus operandi*. I hated his 'new man' pose. Connie told me all about it, the way he massaged her with aromatic oils before sex (I'd never done that for her – it showed what a slob I was), the way he kissed her toes, nibbled her ears, tongued her navel and, finally, on the back of this caring massaging bullshit would persuade her into freaky positions from the *Kamasutra*. Amazing how creative blokes could be when it came to the challenge of pinching another man's woman.

But that's the trouble with bullshit. We hate to see it working for anyone else. Couldn't he have tried it on with another girl. Why Connie? He knew about me, but he didn't feel guilty. It seemed like he wanted to fuck me up as much as he wanted to simply fuck Connie. He was determined to write me out of the picture, telling Connie how useless I was, how two-faced, boring and unreliable. I just used her as a convenient, regular shag, but he wanted to worship her womanhood.

She'd been on Tom's motorbike, clinging to him, breathing in his smells of leather and Eternity as they roared down country lanes. His parents were easy-going. Tom and Connie could make love as much as they wanted to and sit at the breakfast table the next morning without a blush.

And now she was knitting him a jumper.

At first, when I was still treating it as a joke, she'd reassured me that his prick wasn't as big as mine, now she said she'd only been trying not to hurt my feelings. It was bigger and better. Even the sight of it made her tremble with anticipation. And he knew what to do with it. The dazed and happy look on her face frightened the hell out of me.

God, the great universal hang-up. Cock size. Men were petrified about being found wanting. Virtually every other letter we received at *Razzle* mentioned it somewhere. These men were all proud eight-inchers, they had women trembling with the sheer size of their members.

Why this war of attrition? He'd never met me, didn't even know what I looked like.

Dennis had mocked-up a top shelf in his office. After going out and buying all the rival mags, he lined them up on the ledge and strolled along by them, right to left, left to right, putting himself in the punter's place. What would catch his eye? Then he rearranged the order. What if the punter came to *Mayfair* first? He might never get as far as *Razzle*!

Covers were vital he kept telling me. A firm pair of boobs, a lacy red camisole, a lipsticked smile, all those were proven temptations.

One thing Dennis had never trusted me with was cover lines. These snappy four- or five-word come-ons were vital to attract the punter. Short and horny was the formula. Verbal hooks like 'tits' or 'shag' or 'fuck' were strictly forbidden, so it was necessary to get maximum effect from the choices left. 'Sex' always worked. 'Hot' was another good one. Nothing of more than two syllables. 'Horny' was permissible, as were 'randy' and 'raunchy'. Dennis kept telling me the rules, but he never let me have a go, not once. All words had to be on the left, of course, or they might get covered up by the next mag along. Colour was important too. Oranges and greens were useless. Desmond Morris had worked it all out, what kind of luscious reds

pulled triggers in the male mind, set his thoughts on pouting pink labia and stiff ruby nipples. Once these triggers
were set off, the hapless male reached out for the first ersatz
sex he saw.

Dennis set great store by feedback from the readers. But it
seemed readers were getting wise. They weren't so willing
to suspend belief. Far from regarding themselves as hapless
punters, they'd suddenly realized they were consumers.
Nakedness was no longer enough to keep them loyal, they
wanted style, novelty, value for money. Above all they were
getting sick of seeing the same faces (and the rest) in every
issue:

> I'm afraid that what I've purchased today is a
> magazine full of ugly fish-fannied whores and
> prostitutes. The crap you sell on the bookstalls
> is full of Aids-infested, lesbian-looking, over-
> weight prostitutes. Here's my verdict on your
> so-called girls.
> MARIE: Pretty girl. Shame her column is all
> bullshit and lies and she's as gay as a parrot.
> SUZI: Where is her cunt? Because her face, tits
> and body are fucking awful.
> STELLA: No body, no nipples, no face, no
> cunt. A total washout.
> LOLA: This is either a sixty-year-old whore, a
> transvestite or a bad sex change. Or a sixty-
> year-old lesbian with syphilis.
> LYNN: Who's the retired arm-wrestler?

The rest of us nominated this one for our Best Letter of
the Year Award. But Dennis was devastated. For him there
was no ironic interpretation. Complaining letters were out-
numbered a hundred times by compliments. But there was
something about the neatly tabulated all-encompassing nas-
tiness of this one that really dented his confidence.

8 Soho Stories: Part Two

Connie was still seeing Tom, but I suspected things weren't as brilliant as she made out. She'd enjoyed the flattery, the leathery eroticism of the motorbike burn-ups, the energetic shagging – but when it came to it she had too much sense to burn her bridges. I'd been a good friend these past two years and, apart from the embargo on sex, nothing had really changed. We saw each other as much as ever. Just Platonic, that's all it'd be now, she told Tom. But it was a male thing. Platonic or not, he wanted to see me off, hence the ultimatum: me or him.

'See,' I said, 'he treats you like you're his private property. You're not going to stand for that, are you?'

Secretly I'd been hoping that Tom would turn out to be fond of slapping women about. Or have unacceptable kinks – worse than exotic coupling – bondage or rubber fetishism or something. But possessiveness would do to start off the charge sheet. For an independent girl like Connie, such attitudes were a big no-no. I had to be careful though: looking too smug about his sins could blow my advantage. Any hint of 'I told you so' and she'd invert it all: Tom was only being protective, his jealousy proved he really loved her, etc.

Then, one evening, Connie came round to my bedsit, walked straight to the hi-fi and put on a tape. REO Speed-wagon – 'Can't Fight This Feeling'. A well-rehearsed gesture: the tape had been carefully rewound to start with the first notes of the song. It was obvious: Tom had blown her out. She'd pleaded, but he'd had his fuck – and, since she was another bloke's woman, Connie counted as a double-bonus score. As soon as he'd got her to himself he'd have ditched her anyway.

I got quite weepy, because it reminded me of that final scene in *Brief Encounter*, the one where the dopey husband, tashed and tubby, says: 'You've been a long way away. Thank you for coming back to me.' We hugged, I made sympathetic noises. But a good film director would have panned in, over the shoulder, to my satisfied smile.

I'd never paid that much attention to the adverts in *Razzle*, but the production editor's job involved giving them a quick scan for mistakes. They exerted a pervy fascination, especially the classifieds. The real clues to the male agenda lay not with the naked girls, the dirty jokes or the boastful letters, but here in this sexual *Exchange & Mart*. Shrewd operators could make a steady living exploiting men's foibles. Porn videos, massages, photographs, models, dating, threesomes, accommodation, used knickers, even introductions to satanism. And the temptations came from such unlikely places too, not the seedy backstreets of run-down cities, but from the heart of middle-class England. Like the producers of Readers' Wives videos, based in Frinton, a town allegedly so frigidly old-fashioned they still considered pubs as common. Yet here they were, bribing hard-up women to get their knickers off:

> Attractive female models 18–45 for our *Readers'*
> *Wives Striptease Videos*. Experience not needed.
> Send recent topless or nude photo and brief biographical details.

Poverty had always been easy to exploit. Likewise frustration and loneliness:

Seeking an Oriental partner? Or just a sexy
adventure. Send £5 for our latest hot 'n' horny
contact mag.

Somewhere in the Philippines destiny pointed its crooked
finger at some nubile teenager. These girls thought they
were escaping the slums, finding love, but they were on
offer as playthings, one more purchasable service for men
lucky enough to live in a strong economy, men who were
too ugly or too timid to try it on with the local girls. Instead
they could buy their women by mail order, a twentieth-
century version of slavery.

Businessmen (and businessladies), quacks and charla-
tans, the lonely and frustrated, voyeurs and exhibitionists,
the mad, the bad and the dangerous, they were all here.
Sentimental patriots see Britain as a watercolour, a country
cottage in a winding lane. Yet behind its painted door and
curtained windows, who knows what might be lurking?:

Friendly naturist couple offer bed and break-
fast. Single men welcome. £20.00.
Male stripper, inexperienced but enthusiastic.
Extremely cheap.
Fancy a holiday in Ireland? Free accommoda-
tion for single females.

They looked like the kind of ads a serial killer might
have inserted to trap the unwary. Hopelessly direct and
laughably implausible, they still cost £5 a word. If they
didn't work, even occasionally, why did anyone bother
with the expense of inserting them month in month out?

At one time I even considered an ad of my own. One of
Razzle's photographers reckoned he'd made over £300 from
selling 'genuine used knickers' to punters – £10 a pair, plus
£1.50 p&p. I didn't need the money, but like rich folk who
go shoplifting, I fancied the thrill of petty crime, getting
away with a scam. With panties as cheap as 50p a pair in

Berwick Street market (even less if you bought in bulk) how could you fail? All I had to do was scrumple them up, stuff them in Jiffy bags and wait for the cheques to roll in.

The photographer thought I should be more imaginative. For a 30 per cent share of the loot he'd persuaded his girl-friend to part with a jugful of piss and they spent an afternoon in rubber gloves, dunking and squeezing, dabbing the crotches with a pee-soaked sponge to provide a stain of authenticity, as it were. No way would Connie get involved in anything so sleazy. I suggested doing it myself, but the photographer counselled otherwise: serious knicker fetishists could easily tell the difference between male and female urine. Certain to be rumbled by such connoisseurs, I abandoned the idea as a non-starter.

0898 sex-lines were the latest catchpenny craze. Until the 1980s, the most excitement phones could offer was Dial-A-Disc; four kids crammed in a box fighting for a turn at the earpiece to hear a cheerfully lo-fi blast of 'Rocket Man' or 'Jeepster'. Anyone desperate for a female voice could always ring the oddly named TIM, where a robotic woman intoned the passing seconds of our frustrated youth. ('At the third stroke it will be six-thirteen and twenty seconds . . .') We could always tell when a heavy breather had been in: the panes were all steamed up and the phone mouthpiece was beaded with condensed breath. Lingering was inadvisable. You might catch something: a cold at least; VD, some said. Or worse, as happened to me once, the cops could come screeching up in a Panda and accuse you of being the pervert in question!

0898 customers didn't have to take such risks. Their old-fashioned pleasures had been newly labelled Fun! Fun! Fun! When it was 10p a time in the local call-box they called it a crime; now the cost was tripled and, to make it OK for credit-card holders, the hygienic euphemism 'service industry catering for a sophisticated adult market' was adopted.

The choice was, and still is, bamboozling. One panel full

of numbers was blatantly labelled: 'All Sexually Frustrated Men: Ring After 9 p.m.' 'Nymphos In The Nick', 'Nurses Night Out', 'Unfaithful Wives' – there seemed to be a whole parallel world out there. Harmless fun? Or a disturbing insight into the male psyche? What else are we to make of phone lines such as 'Up Auntie's Knickers', 'Spying Through the Kitchen Window' or 'Other Men's Wives'? 'Hot Sex'. 'Deep Sex'. 'Raw Sex'. 'Hard Sex'; there's any sex you like but real sex. You can even get 'Oral Sex for Men'. By phone?

Punters are desperate to believe, but in their heart of hearts they must know it's a con, the breathtaking scale of it matched only by the breathtaking profits. 'Lines are for entertainment purposes only' runs the microscopic warning along the edge of a typical advert. These girls aren't listening, they've done their recording and long since gone home. It's just you and a tape whirring its way through the machine. Ghosted and metallic, these girls are as sexy as the TIM woman. Even the sighs sound pathetic, about as lusty and orgasmic as a pensioner breathing on her spectacles. The only realistic groan comes from the punter's own mouth, when he gets his phone bill.

Despite my qualms, I couldn't deny I was doing well out of the titillation trade. With freelance work on top of my salary, the money piled up faster than I could spend it. Connie was back, the sun shone; life was good. I'd jump off the 159 bus in Regent Street, head for the Barclays cash machine, jab in my PIN and skip away with a handful of dosh. What more could I ask for? For a kid from a Midlands council estate, to be still youngish and living in London, tuned in, connected, creditworthy, seemed like a big enough prize.

The Piccadilly Circus Wimpy was already open, pumping out its aroma of grease and ketchup. Behind it, in Soho proper, the smells of coffee and fresh pastries beckoned. And in the spaces in between lay the intoxicating pong of diesel. These unlikely molecules blended themselves into a perfume: Big City, *parfum de Londres*. I loved it. So what if I had to lie and dissemble, reinvent myself as some vague figure in the media? It wouldn't always be like that. I'd repent, escape, move on. One day.

Guy had a job at Columbia Pictures, just around the corner in Wardour Street. Originally sent there by a temping agency, in a couple of weeks he'd charmed his way from photocopying minion to publicity assistant. We met for lunch two or three times a week. Firstly at McDonald's, Pizzaland or a greasy spoon, then, when we realized we had a bit more money, we decamped to posher places: the Melati, La Verde Valle, the Rasa Sayang. Starvation rations in Belsize Park seemed a long way behind. Had we really lived for a week on sheets of lasagne stolen from Conrads, boiled way beyond any definition of *aldente* and smeared with Daddies sauce for taste? (And once memorably used Parmesan for cheese-on-toast only to see it suddenly burst into flames?)

Our bill arrived on a saucer. I glanced at it and put down the American Express card with a confident snap. I'd watched the way they did it on TV and practised my technique till I got it right.

But not everyone coveted these plastic prizes. My *Razzle* colleagues took the piss relentlessly. Mac the Socialist made his contempt quite clear:

'Pretentious tosser.'

I laughed off the judgement. It rankled though. Boasting about having an Amex was childish, but no more so than crowing about a pools win, and to me that was more or less what it represented: a triumph over the odds. It didn't mean I'd become a loadsamoney Tory-voting convert.

Mac wasn't convinced. He thought my attitude stank.

'I'd rather be a poor tulip than a rich hogweed,' he said, rather poetically.

Tina, the circulation manager's secretary, who I'd never really got on with, also sided with Mac, but for reasons of her own. My loyalty to the Melati irritated the hell out of her.

'Chicken in peanut sauce? What kind of fucking meal is that when it's at home?'

That I preferred Singaporean cuisine to a fry-up or a pizza merely confirmed her suspicions of me as a Brit-knocking culinary traitor. To persuade her otherwise, I even offered to take her out one lunchtime.

'I wouldn't come out with you. I can't stand snobs.'

'Snob?'

'You think you're so great, don't you? You and your fucking la-di-da Mozart crap.'

For a few weeks that summer an odd trade flourished between the empires of Paul Raymond and Marshall Cavendish, the part-works publisher in Old Compton Street. In return for copies of *Razzle* and *Club*, the lads in the Marshall Cavendish warehouse would swap us *Great Composers* (often including a free cassette) and *Microwave Magic*. Courier duties were down to me, since I was the one with the connections (having worked there during my temping days). The whiff of freebies had an intoxicating effect. Everyone in the office suddenly acquired classical leanings.

'Get us Tchaikovsky's *Piano Concerto*,' said Colin. 'I love that first movement.'

'I need *Microwave Magic* parts six and seven,' said Mac. 'And can you get me a binder, if they've got one?'

A list was vital to avoid confusion. Some requests were harder to supply.

'Have they got that one that goes Da-da-dee, da-da-da, di-di, diddly diddly dee?'

'Fuck knows.' I didn't have the patience to play Name That Tune.

Sailing boldly through Marshall Cavendish's front door with a porn-stuffed Jiffy bag wasn't advisable. I went the back way, down the alley that ran from Wardour Street to Dean Street, ducking in through a door alongside the company's loading bay. This fraud had a protocol of its own. Chatting about cricket, weather, holiday plans, we studiously avoided mentioning the business in hand. I never said what I'd come for and they never asked. After a cup of tea and a bikky, I left my bag of *Razzle* behind and sauntered across to the shelves of magazines. The bag disappeared, and a blind eye was turned while I thieved all the goodies on my shopping list.

Despite monthly sales in the millions, it is amazingly hard to find anyone who'll confess to buying girlie mags. Men dread anyone thinking they're hard-up for sex, that they spend good money on wanking aids. The mags are always someone else's. They've been passed on, found on a bus or in an ex-employee's locker ('See, I told you he was a bit pervy!'). Looking is OK though, even *de rigueur*. Together, in the warehouse or the workman's hut, it's a laugh. 'Look at the tits on this . . . Like to get your nose in her bush, Jack? . . . Ted's a black knickers man, ain't you, Ted? . . . Get one of them vibrators for the missis . . .' Frustration, loneliness, desperation, these are the real subtexts that run beneath the laughter and the jokes. But such weaknesses are taboo. Each of these men knows they wank; they know the others wank; but it's something grown men just don't talk about. At any one time tens of millions of girlie mags and porn videos are in circulation, but the freemasonry is so solid that tracing the real owners is virtually impossible.

Every now and then, in the papers, some bloke is demonized as 'Pervert of the Month'. With a hate figure to focus on, the country is united in its contempt – and the rest of the girlie-mag readers breathe a sigh of relief. They've escaped the spotlight again.

Les was on his way back to Australia, to be a teacher. Hopefully no one down under would ever find out about his stint in porn, now conveniently lost on his CV, laundered, ironed and neatly folded into the phrase 'various casual work whilst travelling around Europe'. Grape-picking, bar work, looking after a petrol pump, that's what people would think of. Who'd imagine, at a shirt-and-tie interview, that he'd spent his time at a typewriter coining new euphemisms for vaginas and pricks? When he chatted to mums and dads on parents' night, how would they guess that this was the man who gave the world such inventive phrases as 'lust groove', 'love slot' and 'spunk truncheon'?

See, I told myself: though Les obviously had a good laugh with his work, he'd pulled back in the end. Porn was as easy to pick up as any routine clerical task, but didn't have to be a permanent job, or an irreversible state of mind. Reinventing yourself was easy. You were under no obligation to confess your past. Once you'd made your mind up to move on, you just did it.

A farewell piss-up was the order of the day. In the pub on his last afternoon Les reached out to say goodbye, totally forgetting he had a fresh pint of Castlemaine in his hand-shaking hand. Crash! Customers who didn't get soaked by the spume of XXXX spent the rest of their lunch-hour inspecting every mouthful of chilli for needles of glass.

The toilet beckoned, and I don't remember much after that, except that when I returned Les was nowhere to be seen. Still, the image of that pint in free-fall remains to this day, as timelessly amusing as Chaplin eating his boot.

I knew Julie had been pregnant when our affair ended. People saw the evidence, put two and two together and gave me sly sidelong looks. 'Julie's up the stick, then.' I hated the way grudging admiration was coupled with that horrible phrase. Some people thought getting her 'up the stick' was the crowning act of a daredevil escapade. I'd had the fun, and left Mervyn to pick up the tab. But I wasn't proud of what I'd done. In *Razzle* and *Fiesta* it happened every day: other men's wives were being fucked left, right and centre by the heroes of girlie-mag culture, the Jack-the-lads with their eight-inch pricks and their love 'em and leave 'em mission. But the fun stopped with ejaculation, the rest of the story was always censored. According to the boys' charter you were allowed to admit fathering bastards, but never to be a father.

For the publishers of girlie mags, censorship had always been a giant bugbear. In the USA they cynically invoked the Constitution to protect their 'freedom of speech'. Here in Britain they use the 'generation gap' ploy. Only old biddies and crusty churchgoers objected to sex, people having fun; ergo liberals had a choice between siding with the killjoys and prudes or, if not exactly approving of it, then defending pornography as an adult choice.

Of course, when it came to it, girlie mags were the biggest censors of all, jailers to a hundred thousand women without voices.

Mervyn knew the baby wasn't his, but he'd never admit it. In the Midlands culture of the seventies it was better to take on a shitty-nappied cuckoo than lose face. If anyone was a hero, he was.

When I left to live in London I carried the guilt with me. But greater, always, was the feeling of loss. On my table in Belsize Park stood a photo I'd managed to get hold of: a small boy on a swing. Scant consolation. Like the punters, I too was condemned to stand at the edge of a two-dimensional world, yearning for affection. I lived a sad fantasy. No matter how long I looked at a picture and wished, that swing would always be beyond my reach. I'd never get a chance to push it, have a laugh.

Then, one day, a bolt from the blue. A letter from Derbyshire Social Services. It seemed that Julie and Mervyn had split up years back and Martin had been taken into care. The idea tortured me. All those fine ideals of mine – caring for kids, acting decent – all bullshit. It wasn't really my fault, but when it came down to it I'd done no better than the other fuckers on the piss and the pull on Friday nights, those men I despised, the idiots who played Russian Roulette, but with sperm instead of bullets.

Now he was eleven, Social Services deemed it high time

Martin learned about me, and suggested that I drop him a line. So began a flurry of letters: I told him I was a journalist, working for magazines, living in a nice flat. One of *Razzle*'s suppliers had recently given me a bottle of posh brandy, so, drunk on that, I dabbed away self-pitying tears and shamelessly tried all the flimsy excuses I could think of. What the hell was I babbling about? he must have wondered. How could I expect him to understand? He wanted a dad, not a wimp.

'Lætitia? I'm afraid she's not here at the moment.'

Paul Raymond's payroll listed no one by the name of Lætitia. Nor was there a Bernice, Hattie or Tiffany. They were all aliases of Penny, *Razzle*'s latest assistant editor. Her evening job in a wine bar brought her in touch with all kinds of loners and chancers. They were mostly respectable yuppie types: accountants, lawyers, shop managers. But Penny saw through the pose: take away the shirts and ties, the bleepers and Filofaxes, and these men had exactly the same agenda as randy brickies. To palm them off she jotted the number of our direct line on a napkin, along with one of her pseudonyms. Each morning, sitting down at her typewriter, she issued a bulletin of likely interruptions.

'If anyone calls on the green phone, I'm not here. Unless it's someone called Alan. If it's a guy called Tony, tell him I don't work here any more.'

Mac and I quickly got used to fielding these calls from would-be suitors, gaining along the way some shocking insights into Bromley nightlife. In a short while we knew who was shagging who, who was a wanker and who was a hunk, and though we'd never seen any of these people we became as attached to their fates as if they'd been characters in *The Archers*.

I took to Penny straight away. Not romantically, but like a big sister. I liked her independent attitude. The heavy make-up may have made her look like a vamp, but no bloke was going to take her for a ride, literally or metaphorically.

Spunky prose gave Penny no problems either. She had only to imagine what her would-be suitors were after and flesh it out a bit. Even Dennis had to admit that she knew her stuff. He'd been reluctant to take Penny on at first, but because as many women were now applying for porno jobs as men – whatever their reasons – they were a safer bet than many of the oddballs who applied.

When Soho gets hot it gets hot in lots of ways. Along Brewer Street, Rupert Street and Old Compton Street the tarts leave their windows open, desperate for a breeze to blow away the smells of cheap scent and male sweat. When the curtains waft apart it's not unusual to catch sight of a punter with his pants down, whiskery arse pumping away between a pair of well-waxed legs. 'Entertaining' is a round-the-clock activity. Luckless husbands, denied a shag the night before, rush their breakfasts and hotfoot it up to town and a girl can be at work before she's had a chance to clear away the coffee cups and soggy cornflakes.

'Hey, lads, come and look at this!'

Taffy, another of the art-room boys, had only been up in London for a few months, but Soho was everything he'd believed it to be: neon signs, porno films, tarts in fishnets, Maltese pimps beckoning from doorways. This time his eyes were really popping – live porno action. Across the street a wide open window gave us a front-row view of another couple having it off.

'Bloody shameless, innit?' Taffy watched the bum going up and down between the clutching legs. 'Wait till I tell the lads in Swansea. They'll never believe it.'

Value for money was obviously top priority on this punter's checklist: oblivious to his audience in the *Razzle* office he'd been at it for at least fifteen minutes. If Taffy had had a football rattle he'd have been revving it around his head in rowdy encouragement.

'How's that for staying power. Poor bitch'll be bandy-legged for the rest of the day.'

Eventually the man reached his climax, lunging decisively as the tart's legs clamped the small of his back. The dull roar of the Soho traffic muffled his groan, then he collapsed exhausted on top of his partner.

We began to drift away, but Taffy hadn't finished looking: he wanted to see the girl when she got up. He reckoned it was that tart he'd told us about the other day, the one in the leather mini who'd tried to lure him in when he went out to fetch the lads' mid-morning doughnuts.

The punter got up, lit a cigarette and grabbed his shirt from the back of a chair.

'Light one for her, then, you selfish bastard,' muttered Taffy. 'I dunno, no manners some blokes.'

Joke chivalry died on his lips, swamped by a loud groan. Green-faced with horror he watched as a second man got up off the bed and wiped his bum with a handful of Andrex tissues.

'It's a fucking homo!'

The rest of us cackled. A priceless dilemma. Whatever would the lads in Swansea say if they knew Taffy had got a hard-on from watching two gays on the job?

'Fucking homos. Shouldn't be allowed.'

His macho defences were on red alert. This wasn't the kind of gayness he'd always laughed at, limp-wristed *Are You Being Served?* stuff. Far removed from clichés, real-life Soho homosexuality meant penetrative lust, a bit of rough for clerical and middle-management types from Surbiton and Wimbledon. For all we knew, two hours ago, this man had been sitting down for cornflakes and orange juice with his wife and kids.

Taffy glared at us in disbelief. How could we possibly find it funny? We'd known all along, hadn't we? We'd stood by, silently sniggering, and let him make a tit of himself.

'Could have been kids walking past,' he added weakly, fighting for the moral high ground but slipping backwards on an avalanche of clattering pebbles. How could he reconcile his macho cheerleading with the brutal truth?

'Yeah, all those people walking by on stilts,' we agreed.

That spring Guy and I took a two-day trip to Amsterdam. Neither of us had been before and we wanted to see if the place was as wacky, decadent and laid-back as people made out.

Our itinerary featured the Van Gogh Museum (naturally, since we weren't philistines), but it was the city's red-light area we'd really come to gawp at. Compared with London's Soho, the neat streets of Amsterdam's sex zone, decorated with trees, dappled by reflections from the canals, looked refreshingly unseedy. Macs and other disguises weren't necessary. Punters didn't look guilty, nor did they wander around in a daze, as though they'd just been thumped by a baseball bat marked 'swindle'. This sin sector had the genteel, good-natured air of a village fête.

Neither of us had ever been with a prostitute, but we agreed it would be a shame to visit Amsterdam and not get in the spirit. Unlike the high-heeled whey-faced tarts who lurked on the street corners of Leeds and Birmingham, the women here had nice teeth and spoke with soothing Euro accents. None of them said anything as awful as 'Looking for business, love?' but sat in their picture windows reading *Die Welte*. All the same, we stood and dithered, debating the pros and cons: how much would it cost? What about Aids? What if anyone found out?

The woman I chose looked like the blonde in Abba. Flanelling my prick and balls, Anneka was as chatty as a hairdresser doing a pre-cut wash. Where had I come from? How long was I staying? Had I seen the Van Goghs? Van Gogh, oh yes! I seized the chance to show her I was more than just a punter. '*Sunflowers* is great, but I prefer *Cornfield with Cypresses*.' In a flash, mid-sentence, she'd unrolled a condom on me. My prick meant no more to her than an arm held out for a measles jab. She dropped the ripped sachet in a flowery paper basket, on top of two previous ones.

Anneka was gorgeous, no doubt about that, but I took no enjoyment at all. I couldn't shake off an image of myself as a pumping machine, and I couldn't forget that other punters were strolling past only feet away from the bed. They'd be there when she drew back the curtains. The ones waiting and debating, they'd see me coming out, maybe make up their minds by evaluating the width of my smile. I came, not orgasmically, but mechanically, with no sense of anything except a certain squelchy discomfort. Quickly hiding my shrivelled member, I said thank you, Anneka bade me the Dutch equivalent of 'Have a nice day', and that was that. A simple business transaction. I wouldn't have been surprised if she'd given me a receipt.

Guy was waiting outside. 'You could have paid by Visa,' he said, pointing to the sticker discreetly tucked away in the corner of the window. Why then, if it was a service that had the tacit approval of international banking, should I feel ashamed? Anneka was my one and only prostitute in forty years. I'm not proud of it. But admitting it is no trauma either. It's almost meaningless.

An hour later, churning our way along the canals in a hired pedalo, Guy and I made eye contact with two young women in another craft. Now this was more like it: commercial screwing had nothing to compare with the thrills of the chase . . . this was what we both craved, being looked at, fancied, approved of. Paying for sex was no big deal, it was merely a service, but this rush of hope was something you'd never be able to buy.

Somewhere along the way, we made a wrong turning and lost them. Deflated, we paddled our way around, angrily blaming each other for lousy navigation. Then they suddenly appeared again. Off we went, legs pumping madly, kicking up more surge than the speedboat scene in *Puppet on a Chain*. The girls were coasting now. They'd led us a chase, now they wanted us to catch up, start a conversation.

In ten minutes the four of us would be sitting at a canalside café. As triumphant as a coastguard patrol picking up smugglers we surged alongside – only to find two Japanese pensioners, who from their looks of terror obviously thought we were water-based muggers. They grinned nervously and waved a map at us, asking us some directions. I nearly told them to fuck off but, even sexually frustrated, I couldn't forget my manners.

Youth employment has an extra dimension in Amsterdam. Any shortage of engineering apprenticeships can always be offset by opportunities in the sex business. Live sex shows, for instance, where hard-up youngsters can take a step beyond nude modelling, shagging live on stage for an audience of tourists. We went to see one. Just for a laugh, we told ourselves. But how were we any better than the rest of the punters who flew into town for a cheap thrill? We said it was just curiosity, but didn't everyone use the same excuse?

Mac called me Sergeant Mustard, on account of my knitted yellow tie.

'Ye cannae go meeting celebrities in a mustard tie,' he insisted. 'It's a bad impression.'

As part of his process of mixing legit stuff with the titillation, à la *Playboy*, Dennis had instigated the '*Club* Interview', a monthly chat with a celebrity, usually one with a new book or record to push, passed on to me by Colin in his role as *Razzle*'s literary editor.

Geoff, the studio manager from *Fiesta*, had finally broken into full-time photography and even had his own studio. Dennis used him on a freelance basis. One summer morning he and I motored down to Berkshire for a chat with Uri Geller. He was on his exercise bike when we arrived and to save his time I agreed to do the interview as he pedalled. Afterwards he gave us a quick tour of his palatial gardens ('My koi carp are worth £1000 each,' he boasted) and then bent a spoon for us to take away as a souvenir.

Before heading up the M4 we stopped for tea and scones in a quaint café in Sonning village. How wonderful to be one of Uri's neighbours and own an ivy-veiled cottage here. But, if his boasts about the extent of his force field were to be believed, you'd have to put a lead shield around the cutlery drawer.

Next on my list was Kingsley Amis. Meeting a real writer was a great thrill. What a pity I felt like a fraud: he appeared to be under the impression that *Club* was a magazine aimed at members of gentlemen's clubs. I didn't dare correct him.

'Someone once likened your prose to the shock of finding a meat cleaver in a child's cot.' (Colin insisted I slip in this quote from a review.) 'What would be your response to that?'

He eyed me with loathing. 'Who said that?'

I'd forgotten. I wasn't even sure I'd got the quote right anyway. My burbling only served to double his contempt. His publishers made him do these interviews, but he just wanted to get it over with as quickly as possible. On my way out I had the brass to tell him I'd written a novel too.

'A novel?' He stared at me. 'At your age? How old are you, then, twenty-eight? I'm sure it must be brilliant.'

Fooled by his flattery, I missed the sarcasm, didn't even see his look for what it was: total scorn.

Back at my flat I poured a beer, switched on my typewriter and prepared to transcribe the Amis dialogue. Damn . . . I'd put on the wrong side of the tape. I turned it over. That side was blank too, nothing but a continuous low buzzing. It all came back to me: he'd made me so nervous I'd forgotten to press Record.

'Ring him up and get another interview,' ordered Dennis when I confessed my gaffe the next day.

I babbled my explanation, but Kingsley was in no mood for sympathy. The great writer told me in no uncertain terms to get lost.

If I had a favourite it was Justin de Villeneuve, Twiggy's

one-time mentor and boyfriend, who'd just published his autobiography, *An Affectionate Punch*. We met up for coffee and ambled into Hyde Park for a chat.

'I like your shoes,' he said, as we rounded off the questions and answers.

After my experience with Kingsley Amis I treated flattery with caution. But yes, they were dead comfortable, I'd never had a pair as good. He peered at them with an expert eye. Elephant skin, weren't they? 'They make bloody good shoes, elephants do.'

Back at the office my constant name-dropping soon got on everyone's nerves. 'It's just a fucking job,' argued Mac. 'They only meet you because they have to.'

'They're good friends,' I insisted. 'My kind of people. Ray Cooney's going to read my script.'

I'd got myself another agenda now. Hearing about old colleagues on the grapevine – one of *Fiesta*'s art room guys was now Art Editor at *Harpers & Queen*, and even bumbling Clive was working at the *Independent* – I realized I'd dropped miles behind. Each day that passed was one more day in the land of obscurity. The *Club* interviews gave me a chance to compile an alternative CV, a portfolio full of celebrity chat and non-sexual prose. Summoned for an interview, any potential employer could see that not only was I a good writer, but I mixed easily with writers, rock stars and actors.

Despite his forty-a-day habit, Dennis showed no signs of conking out and remained entrenched as top dog. I was in my mid-thirties, Colin was approaching the big Four-O. We could be stuck at Paul Raymond's for years, decades even, frustrated middle-agers bashing out the same old crap, smoking ourselves to an early grave. Paul Raymond wouldn't give a stuff. You could never progress, never develop, because male mythology itself was going nowhere. The letters still arrived by the sackload, those same old shagging stories, mostly, yet lately some had become even more puzzling, their obsessions unsettling:

You seem really like angels. You were the lost
apple in the cider barrel, jugged up by a horny
pig. Girls, I'm a country boy who wants you. I
love the open spaces . . .

I demand more women in men's public lava-
tories, cleaning the urinals. I want more pictures of brazen huzzies in gents' toilets
standing at the urinals. It would make me
wank myself to death. Up the urinals! Now can
a woman piss into a male urinal like a man?
Can you, Dionne, you fucking slut!

Bright staff like Colin, Mac, Penny and me, we surely
had better things to do with our lives than help Paul Raymond make his millions? Bodies as commodities, that was
a bad enough idea, but so were brains chained to production-line values. Porn, titillation, glamour, whatever you
called it, at the end of the day it was a game for young
people. Those kids in the art room were all right: working
for *Razzle* was no bar to a better job. Such a scandalous CV
even had a jokey post-modern gloss: prove yourself with
some clever layouts and they'd gladly have you at *Esquire*
or *Vanity Fair*. On the writing side escape was much harder.
Yet, with Dennis standing over me I'd produced stuff that
was well-crafted, witty and literate. If I'd applied the same
effort on my own behalf I'd have been well away. If I was
the decent writer I thought I was, I could get along without
the patronage of Paul Raymond.

One Friday I caught the train to Derby and went to meet
Martin for the first time. Nicola, his social worker, drove
me to his foster parents' home in her Mini Metro and I sat
in the car while she went in to fetch him. We hit it off
straight away, as if fate had hidden a transmitter on each
of us. Switched off for years, out of contact, as soon as we
got close enough they crackled back to life.

It didn't take me more than a couple of hours to make up my mind: I'd go back home, be a dad, get a job on the local paper, make up for all those years I'd missed out on.

Nicola thought it a brilliant plan. As soon as Social Services had run the usual checks they'd happily give the go-ahead.

Checks?

As soon as they found out what I'd been doing, who I worked for, the game was up. No way would they agree to custody. Some people might think it odd enough already, a single man taking on a young boy, but a background like mine gave it an extra twist. If there were any feminists in the Social Services office they'd be on to me like a shot.

In the event, no one said a thing. The name of Paul Raymond rang no alarm bells. Maybe, like Kingsley Amis, they thought *Club* was a harmless gentlemen's magazine, *Escort* a monthly for car enthusiasts.

But was I fit to be a parent? A man who went on Amsterdam weekends and sat in the front row of sex shows? Who strolled round the Sex Museum laughing at the shape and prodding-power of ancient dildoes? Maybe I ought to confess it all. But no, I still refused to acknowledge that was really me in the plush tip-up seat at the sex show; it was just a stand-in playing at being a wild boy. Amsterdam was a one-off. I'd been there, done it, but I felt no urge to repeat it. Sex shows and prostitutes, however pretty, held no fear of addiction at all.

I nearly blew it though.

Despite Dennis's diktat, we still found half a dozen reasons a day to visit our colleagues in Archer Street. Any excuse for a mosey through the market, a breath of fresh air and bruised fruit. Though wary of upsetting Dennis, I lingered long enough to get a date with Alison, the girl in Accounts.

I just wanted to see if I still had the pulling power. The satisfaction came from seeing how many steps it took to go from a neutral topic to an invitation to potential bedding. Starting with some jokey spiel about bedsit life, about how I could look after myself, how brilliant my cooking was, how I enjoyed cooking but doing it for two was much more fun, etc, etc, Alison accepted my invitation for pasta and a game of Trivial Pursuit, and she came home with me on the 159 after work to make sure I was really cooking it, not trying to trick her with a Sainsbury's ready meal.

We polished off two bottles of Frascati, got rid of our guests and fell into bed. Next morning we were on the 159 back to the West End.

Alison and I had sex only twice before we fell out over something stupid. I wasn't that bothered. A few days later she rang me, but not to apologize for being stubborn, rather to tell me she was pregnant. Possibly. More than likely.

The news scared the shit out of me. I'd really gone and fucked up everything this time. Literally, metaphorically, really.

Martin was over the moon at the prospect of having a real dad at last. I'd descended like a comic-book hero who'd put everything right. But I was a joke. The only comic-book hero I resembled was Bollocksman, a hopeless shit with a one-track mind and bollocks for a brain.

One fuck had ruined everything. Would taking on one child mean deserting another? How the hell would I get out of this one?

For three days I sweated it out. At night I lay awake, tortured by what I'd done. Across on the other side of London those busy cells were already dividing. In a few weeks, the bambino-to-be would have an eye, a tiny nose, stumpy little fingers. I rang Alison on the internal phone and made coded enquiries: had her sister's exam results come in yet?

The baby turned out to be a false alarm. But the shock certainly sobered me up. Not just the narrow escape from catastrophe, but the scary glimpse of time running out. I couldn't, as Jean-Paul Sartre put it, live my life between parentheses. These affairs weren't trivial amusements, detached from real life, they were dangerous games. Unlike some blokes, I'd never consciously set out to acquire a track record, but now I looked back at the past seven years, the twenty-one beddings, the numerous flirtations. I saw my life for what it was: not a great success by any means, just a haphazard sequence of substitutes.

I didn't want to get all pious and hypocritical, but for me at least I knew the best option was growing up a bit.

9 Final Days and Home

Dennis had been having a recurring dream. Back from lunch one day, he found the office deserted, a bureaucratic *Marie Celeste*, phones ringing unheeded, time's dust falling on the typewriters.

Those lazy, noodle-scoffing, good-for-nothings!

Two steps at a time he stormed up the stairs to the roof, sure his staff would be out sunbathing. Instead he found Paul Raymond, standing at the edge, lazily urinating on to the street below. Puzzled tourists shook out their pac-a-macs and snapped up umbrellas to ward off the unseasonal shower. Dennis sizzled with indignation. It was high time someone took a stand and, dammit!, this was the moment and he was the man. On the pavement below knots of people were already gathering, staring up at the roof-top drama: Punter's Champ versus Wicked Porn Baron.

Then Dennis woke up, shouting: 'You're not pissing on the little man any more, Mr Raymond!'

What did it mean? Colin and I, in Dennis's office for our usual pre-work natter session, shrugged helplessly. Apart from donning stick-on goatees and pretending to be kindly analysts, what else could we do?

'Too much cheese for supper,' Colin suggested.

Dennis glared. Flippancy was no response.

As a dream it hardly rated alongside the big-time visions of John Bunyan or Martin Luther King, yet it turned out to be eerily prophetic. A few days later the switchboard girl put through a summons from the real Paul Raymond.

As I saw him weave through the fruit sellers Dennis,

returning from the meeting, cast a shadow over the flirta-
tious gaiety of Soho, a thin black storm cloud choked with
rain and thunder. I dodged back from the window. A
purely Pavlovian reflex. I knew, from the way he walked,
that excuses were no longer necessary. Back at my desk, I
tapped meaningless rows of letters on the typewriter, just
to make a noise, to look as if I was doing something. Anything but wait in silence.

Dennis's shadow fell across the paper, but I didn't turn,
I couldn't bear to meet his eyes. What could I say – 'Hi,
Dennis, how'd it go, then?' I felt tense enough for a coron-
ary. And half wished for one, just to relieve the tension.
Thirty seconds he must have stood there, yet no one in the
office said a thing. Then the shadow lifted. When he'd gone
I had a giggling fit. I couldn't help it.

Paul Raymond wanted a younger readership for *Club*,
something more upbeat. Readers' Wives had already been
banned and '*Club* Comic', with its line-up of boozy blue-
jokers from the brown-ale saloons of Doncaster and Gates-
head was just as plebeian. As for my so-called celebrity
interviews – who gave a shit about old buffers like Donald
Sinden and Kingsley Amis anyway? An old spoon-bender
like Uri Geller had little credibility as a role model for the
young men of the eighties. Classy birds, streetwise chat,
alternative jokes, that's what these young males wanted,
and Paul Raymond was determined to provide it, to reassert
his position as the benign godfather of titillation.

Club should have been an international brand, a style
accessory for men who drove Ferraris and sipped
Budweiser, not a wanking mag for the working classes. (Its
small-print warning: 'NOT FOR SALE TO MINORS' should
have continued: 'NOR MEN WHO SMOKE WOODBINES/
DRIVE FORD CORTINAS/WEAR ANORAKS.') Girlie mags
had had post-modernism – Readers' Wives, shag tales from
the backstreets and editorial irony were a departure from
the dolly-bird fantasy world of old – now it was time for
a return to traditional values. Club – the very word came

pre-loaded with notions. Paul Raymond obviously preferred the smooth translation (Canadian Club, Club Class,
gentlemen's club), the exclusive jet-set to which every guy
in jockeys aspired. But I'd never been able to shake off the
TV jingle of a few years previous: 'If you like a lot of
chocolate on your biscuit join our club.'

The coup had been carefully planned. Within a day of
Dennis's departure *Club* was in the hands of a fast-tracking
young turk with a trendy haircut. And Colin got *Razzle*.
With Dennis gone, a new laid-back regime came into force.
We could buy cold beers from the off-licence next door,
take our typewriters up on the roof. As long as the work was
done, no one cared how long we lingered in the Chinese or
the Hayward Gallery. Ideal working conditions, but too late
for me. I'd handed in my notice weeks ago. I couldn't
change my mind. And didn't want to. I'd seen enough tits
to last a lifetime.

Apart from Dennis, whose opinion hardly mattered now,
my decision to leave had been readily blessed. Especially
by the female staff. Sweets kept appearing on my desk, like
glittering rewards, and phrases like 'an honourable man'
were muttered in a self-conscious way.

Others looked at it less soppily. 'Nice to see a man facing
up to his responsibilities,' they said. I hated the smugness
of that, as if I'd run away and was now being frog-marched
back to face the music.

Going home. It's a phrase that oozes country 'n' western
sentiment. Hear the mournful glissando of the slide guitar,
see that manly tear. But, for me, small-town life held no
such fond memories. The move was purely practical – a
four-bedroom house for £18,000, for one thing. I had to
think of Martin's welfare too: plucking him from a village
school and throwing him in with the streetwise kids of
Camden would have been a cruel misjudgement. They'd
have eaten him.

That final summer in London had sadness at all its edges.
The skies were golden all right, but they had an imperfect

second-hand quality, as if God had made them from smoothed-out toffee wrappers. For old times' sake I visited the Belsize Tavern and stayed for a pint. But I felt ill at ease. Scared even, by the way time had passed, so much of it, so quickly. Dispensing Guinness and Fosters in twinkling glasses with nary a dribble, the young barmen looked spookily professional and wore ties with brewers' logos. The drama students, nurses and au pairs were still there – just as penniless, just as pretty – but they all seemed spoken for. Somewhere in NW3, in another flat, was another Nick, another Guy; maybe they were these lads behind the bar. It all belonged to them now – these years, these girls, even the songs on the jukebox, by bands I'd never heard of.

By the time my cigarette had burned down I was itching to go. Abandoning my beer, mouthing silent goodbyes, all I took away were some memories.

I crossed the road to the launderette in the vague hope of seeing Carol, pretty, *retroussé* nose stuck in a maths book while her freshly Daz'd knickers tumbled daintily in the drier. But she'd passed her finals now and I'd seen her name listed in the Glittering Prizes section of *The Times*. I'd never had her, but still, the sense of loss was unbearable. She'd already gone, moved on, set up a double-income yuppie home with spotty Quentin. There'd be no more public knicker displays now that they had their own private Zanussi.

In the cartoons, when you need a quick fix, you send off to Acme Inc. for the appropriate kit. Next day a Looney Toons postman (just his legs as a rule) leaves a box on your doorstep. The Instant French Kit, for instance, comes with a beret, stripy T-shirt, accordion and baguette. I sent for Instant Parenthood. What a con! Apart from a can of chalk dust for greying your hair and some throat lozenges for when you'd shouted yourself hoarse, the box was empty. Except for a sheet of instructions with the message: make it up as you go along! Funding school uniforms, assessing

reports, lectures about smoking, birds-and-bees pep talks –
it all had to be improvised.

But it wasn't so bad. I got a job on the local paper, bought
a computer, made up my mind I'd get down to some serious
writing, finish that novel, find an agent.

My old pals were still around. Fatter, balder, sadder.
Even wiser in some cases. While I'd been chatting up drama
students and French au pairs in the Beer & Curry, they'd
plodded along regardless, working, boozing, fucking.

Births. Marriages. Deaths – the old gang had figured in
all three sections of the local rag. And a new one had
recently been invented, just for them, those piss-taking ads
put in by spouses and workmates:

Rick Smith
is 40 Today!
Happy Birthday
You Old Swinger!

That feather-cut, those flares, that kipper tie! Hilarious
stuff, supposedly, but for me it hardly raised a smile. On
the contrary, I found these old snapshots unbearably sad.
Why did people have this urge to laugh at what they'd
been? Having lived in 1973 was no crime. The lads with
the haircuts and big-collared shirts looked clean, decent,
full of optimism. Chasing girls, bopping to T. Rex and Slade,
going to smutty films, flipping through *Mayfair* and *Fiesta*.
Easy to please, no side to them, they'd been OK in those
days.

Then, one day, it had all fallen into place – sex, women,
efficient lying – that's when the trouble started. Generations
of trouble. In the years I'd been away, Rick had fathered half
a dozen kids. As survivalist procreation, on the blunderbuss
principle, he deserved the Queen's Award for Industry.
And initiative, because it was all off his own bat. He hadn't
got the idea from girlie mags or been corrupted by porno
films. Rick was one of the few who spurned that stuff. He

needed no lessons and looked up to no mentors – he had a natural flair.

When Rick fathered his first bastard there'd been mutterings of envy and approval. The consensus was that the jammy sod was getting so much bed he'd forgotten how to walk (and his bit on the side was a fit sixteen-year-old schoolgirl too!). People made envious jokes about sowing wild oats.

Hypocrisy? At the end of the day, was Rick any different from Guy? Or me, come to that? Yes, he was clumsy and stupid. But it wasn't an endearing clumsiness. Nor was it really accidental. We had reams of rules about pornography and stripping and indecent exposure, but we still hadn't legislated to prevent this parody of fatherhood. Rapists and child-molesters weren't the only ones who ought to be castrated – what about those dopey arseholes who couldn't walk down the street without stopping to knock up some seventeen-year-old?

What baffled me most was the women. They despised men for buying girlie mags, yet excused people like Rick as lovable rogues. So, he had a nice smile, sheep's eyes, pop-star hair, but couldn't they see he was a liability? And for every Rick, there's a hundred more, all cloned off the same small-town template. And for every woman who condemns these Jack-the-lads, there's always another one who reckons she'll be the one to keep him. Rather like those boxing booths at the circus: dupes kept coming up for a go, but no one was ever going to win.

Somehow, someway, I knew our tight-assed provincial burg had to share the blame. Burton-on-Trent is typical of any small town in Britain. You only had to look at its frigid history to see something was up.

BANNED! Back in 1973 the local bigwigs were so frightened of the corruptive powers of the *Last Tango in Paris*, they quickly passed a by-law to stop it being shown. It still hasn't been, and because of this, locals still think of the film as the height of depraved sex.

212

BANNED! The naturist massage parlour. 'OWNER ASKS JOB APPLICANTS TO STRIP!' read the headlines in the local paper. After the inevitable protests and a legal kerfuffle, the town hall clerks said the owner was quite within his rights. But the cops raided him anyway and charged him with living on immoral earnings. Opening up in the High Street was his big mistake. He'd have had plenty of customers otherwise, but no one wanted to step out of a massage parlour straight into the busiest street in town!

BANNED! The Chippendales. One or two pubs in Burton are allowed to have topless barmaids. One even boasts a lunchtime stripper (Sunday lunchtimes at that). But the harmless frolics of baby-oiled hunks are definitely not on. 'It's not a rule banning people from removing clothing,' said a local official. 'It specifically refers to striptease-style entertainments.' Why the big hang-up about pricks? Was someone frightened of women seeing a series of limp concertina'd chipolatas? To maintain its mythic status a prick has to stay invisible. The real offence of the man fined for peeing in a shop doorway was nothing to do with public health (dogshit and litter are a natural part of the townscape), more because someone might have seen his member.

Though Rick still had it off here and there, no one took much notice any more. The cement of male solidarity had long since crumbled away, leaving individuals stranded on their own islands of maleness, quirky one-man kingdoms, each with its own moral codes, its own hi-fi collection and its own obscenity laws. Like Rick they had the urges, but they knew that affairs weren't worth the trouble.

Ted had tried adultery – 'redhead, mate, randy little spitfire!' – but since it meant a fidgety existence in a rusting mobile home he soon jacked it in and returned to his wife and kids.

One day, not long after I'd got back, he invited me round

to his house for a video show. In the Midlands at that point, pre-cable TV, you had to know a bloke. Fat Ken let's call him. For £6 he'd rent you two VHS 180s for a week. It was a lucky dip. You could get a full three hours of hot sex; but it was just as likely to fizzle out halfway through, to be replaced by a Midlands news from 1988 and an old episode of *Rising Damp*. Some tapes had been copied so many times they were knackered, the flesh tones disintegrated into smudged orange and puce, nipples pixillated into bizarre brown cubes. But, like everything else to do with sex, all complaints were received with a 'tough luck' shrug.

Was this all there was? A weekly boy's night: four cans of Hofmeister, one hour of trainspotting videos, one hour of porn. I had no stomach for it. The muddy fucking and Germanic grunts were bad enough, but my viewing companions took it as an excuse to embrace me, take me into the male fold. I hadn't wanted to go in there twenty years ago; now, more than ever, as I approached forty, I fought against it even harder. I still lived in hope, but these men had been done down. Middle-age brought a weary cynicism, fuelled by years of marriage, rows, ill-fated affairs, years of rejection, divorce payments. They still fancied their chances with the barmaid in their local, but they'd never do anything about it.

They were just kidding themselves. Their sexual heyday was ages back, as distant and nostalgic as Slade at number one. Now they had grey hair, bald patches, missing teeth and even the sweat which had once been light, spicy and macho had gummed and soured, become a gossamer body-stocking for middle-age.

All the same, I didn't despise them. Perhaps porn was just a part of a natural cycle. You started off with it, enjoyed the real thing for a while, then drifted back to it. But why? These men knew what a naked woman looked like. It had to be something more than simple visual stimuli. My own theory had it as desperate optimism. Wanking over *Razzle* and *Fiesta* wasn't purely mechanical. Could anyone really think that five sad minutes with a tart was the pinnacle of ambition for these men? A spiteful and patronizing verdict. These men weren't as mercenary and phallocentric as feminists made them out to be. Yes, they wanted to fuck, desperately, sadly. But they also craved companionship, cuddles, kisses, warmth. They wanted dates and phone calls and weekends in hotels. Since many of these things were now out of bounds to them, they had to make do.

For all the sad pleasures of these homely porno sessions, these men had done no one any harm. It wasn't the ones with the videos and girlie mags who'd had a string of illegitimate children. By and large they'd stuck to their commitments, seen their kids through school, stuck by their wives, been decent husbands and kind fathers. Their wives, also older and wiser, no longer jealous, didn't entirely disapprove of their husbands' porno comforts. It wasn't hardcore, kinky stuff and at least it stopped them wandering.

None of these options appealed to me, however. I fancied going out on the town, but an unspoken curfew operated on anyone over thirty-five. You just couldn't do it, didn't do it, not unless you wanted to look like a sad old swinger. To enjoy that kind of lifestyle you needed a certain infrastructure, which only being young could give you. A middle-aged man was required to surrender politely to fate: dowdy clothes, beer belly and video sex.

Passing through the newsagent's recently, gazing up at the top shelf, I couldn't believe how many girlie mags there are now. Some shops have dozens, scores of titles I've never even heard of – *Heat*, *Big Mamas*, *Long Legs*, *Rapier* – all neatly overlapped to show glimpses of nipples and naughty words. I couldn't help an urge to take down a *Razzle*, just to see what they were up to. The lady who kept the shop didn't disapprove, she was used to the shifty behaviour of middle-aged men and made a welcome profit from it. But I couldn't bear to be classed alongside them. Who'd believe my interest was purely academic? Part of me wanted to boast: 'I used to work on that', but why rake it up now?

No one would have believed me anyway. Ex-journalists don't hang around in newsagents', misty-eyed, accosting members of the public with rambling tales. Men who worked for *Men Only* and *Club* had nice cars and tall blonde girlfriends. They certainly didn't shop in Kwik-Save and travel around by bus.

The girlie-mag scene has changed over the years. With mavericks like Russell Gay long gone, sex has gone corporate. Northern & Shell's have mags like *Penthouse*, *Forum*, *For Women*, but they're just part of a broad portfolio which includes respectable titles such as *OK Weekly* and *The Green Magazine*. You'll never see the bosses of N&S sashaying around Soho in fur coats, flashing gold rings. They aren't porn barons. Sex sells, and that's a good enough reason for publishing sex magazines.

Galaxy made an ill-fated attempt to cash in on the early nineties craze for female porn – soft-focus penises, muscular hunks, naked and relaxed against all manner of unlikely props. Women bought it, but only because it hit the headlines and the media told them they should enjoy men's bodies as much as men had enjoyed theirs for so long. Fair enough, but it was just a craze. There's no such thing as equality of voyeurism. Girlie mags aren't just about pin-ups, they're a monthly gazette of male attitudes, building-site culture, office lechery and forces of chauvinism. A few naked men and women talking dirty wasn't going to upset the status quo.

Paul Raymond kept his distance from it all, quietly salting away his millions. Why risk hard-won cash on passing fads? His success was founded on a formula that dated back to Neanderthal times. After thirty-odd years his Revuebar still played to packed houses and he'd triumphantly taken over long-time rival *Mayfair*. His name kept popping up in the *Sunday Times* richest five hundred, a few notches higher each year, and it's even been hinted that he might be the richest man in Britain. An ardent supporter of Margaret Thatcher, no one doubts that he's worked hard and cleverly for his fortune. But, sadly, his devotion to private enterprise will never be recognized by anyone of importance. At the end of the day, for all his millions, it's satisfying to know that he has the same credibility problem as the rest of his employees. Even if he gave £1 million to Tory party funds and spent his nights handing out soup and sandwiches to the homeless, it wouldn't get him anywhere. No government of any colour is ever going to ennoble a porn entrepreneur.

In the early nineties his daughter, Debbie, died of a drug overdose. Even at that distance it came as a shock, and a spooky one too since it happened in Belsize Park and the boyfriend involved was a friend of mine from the Belsize Tavern. When I last saw him he'd been a small-time businessman with dreams of being rich and successful, but now his sole claim to fame was being the fella of a dead heiress.

Disillusioned with naff videos, Ted recently got hooked up to satellite TV. Not beamed-in Euro porn, as dangerous as rabies according to some, just The Fantasy Channel: soft-core striptease and simulated sex. But at least the quality is reliable. It's harmless and diverting, but so mild I couldn't imagine anyone getting a hard-on. In fact, the only thing that shocked me was a 'day out with the glamour world's top lensmen' feature, in which I recognized one of the photographers from my *Razzle* days – still at it a decade later and, by the look on his face, still enjoying every minute of it.

Colin, Penny and Mac had all escaped the business, so I'd heard, massaging their CVs to hide the *Razzle* stint from the prejudices of prospective employers. But this photographer was untroubled, saw no reason to go legit. And, let's face it, a steady wage in a post-recession world is not something to treat lightly.

I've always kept one eye on the porn debate, a reliable

chestnut, worthy of discussion on serious late-night TV, guaranteed to get the veins popping on raucous shout-ins like *Central Weekend*. But the pornography they condemn is frequently only pictures and four-letter words. They slag off men for being pleased by naked women, but it's a natural pleasure, it doesn't mean you instantly go off and rape someone, or have a sudden urge to bring unwanted children into the world. If girlie mags are evil, just about every male in the country stands condemned.

If there is any obscenity it's already present in our attitudes, our speech, our jokes. It has percolated into our lives in so many ways we scarcely recognize the signs. You can see it on the faces of beaten wives, in the misery of henpecked husbands and abused children. But you can't blame girlie mags for all that. It's the product of poverty, class, deference and exploitation. We can take away the girlie mags and the porn videos, but it won't make a damned bit of difference.

It isn't so much the images of naked women that cause men to go out and rape, but rather the individual's interpretation of stimuli around him. It is impossible to legislate for such contingencies, and impossible to isolate exactly which stimuli cause any one individual to go beyond the norm. The arguments will run and run, and I have no final word, but if the sight of a naked woman is truly the incitement to violence, then what hope is there for any of us, man or woman?

So, generally, while these earnest women in big spectacles denounced the rats who produced and made money from pornography, I went off to make a cuppa, anything to avoid the reminder, the accusing voices that had followed me even into retirement.

On one such occasion I stood in the kitchen, spooning Gold Blend into a cup, feeling low. Then the spoon clattered out of my hand. What the hell was I feeling guilty about? All in all, I seemed to be the least sex-mad person I knew. While I'd kept shamefacedly dumb about my past, the guilty tittering in the background had become a roar of laughter. No one cared a toss now. Sex had become the lingua franca of the nineties.

Back in the 1970s there was a quaint afternoon show called *Mr and Mrs*, in which timid couples were quizzed about each other's habits. Does he prefer his bacon with the rind left on? Does he snore? Has he ever darned a sock? The most *risqué* question was whether hubby wore his vest in bed. In the 1990s version, *Carnal Knowledge*, couples eagerly reveal all: their favourite sex position, whether Mrs (though they're not of course actually married) swallows during oral sex, whether Mr has talented tongue. To illustrate, they chalk primitive cave drawings on a blackboard, matchstick figures with outrageously large pricks and triangular tits. The audience falls about.

During the *Razzle* years I'd always felt sadly inferior to those cleverpusses who worked in TV, envious of their salaries, their golden haloes. But all that time they must have been flicking through *Fiesta*s and *Escort*s and *Razzle*s, nicking all our ideas! The dirty mag has been cannibalized, its themes and language revamped as TV 'for a sophisticated late-night audience'. *Eurotrash*, *Carnal Knowledge*, *The Girlie Show*, *The Good Sex Guide*. Sex, sex, sex. Even the advertisers are in on it. Ever since Cadbury's Flake every other commercial has subtexts of innuendo and sniggery which are supposed to endear it to a post-modern, clued-up audience. I remember my mum watching a Flake advert – all she saw was a woman eating a Flake. So what was wrong with the rest of the viewers?

I'm not shocked by any of this. Merely bored. And angry. Angry at having wasted so much guilt, when all along everyone has been up for a share of the hanky-panky. TV supplies welcome anonymity, no need for risky ventures into top-shelf land. But viewers' obsessions turn out to be every bit as kinky, just as detailed. I hate the hypocrisy. Girlie mags still have pariah status; the mythic man in the dirty mac is kept on a life-support system to take the can when necessary. By claiming a post-modern ironist stance, everyone else is able to get away with it. People only switch on for a laugh, no one takes it seriously, not like those sad wankers who read dirty mags.

Even our local radio station has got in on the act, with *All Night Love* providing smutty gossip in between the records:

'So, tell us, what's your idea of a good night in bed, Linda?'

'Ooh, Graham! That'd be telling.'

'Snuggle up? Get out the baby oil, something like that?'

'Ooh, yes, we do, Graham.'

'He's a surfer, isn't he, your bloke? Do you help him, like, you know, help him polish his surfboard?'

'I do that for him every night, Graham.'

'You need to get a good grip and rub hard, don't you?'

'Oh yes, I've had plenty of practice!'

'Thanks for calling, Linda.'

The book club I joined offered a variety of titillating reads, all veiled with literary respectability. *Sacred Sexuality* (sexuality in religious art throughout history); *Totally Herotica* (an anthology of women's erotic fiction); *The Complete Kama Sutra* (the first modern unabridged translation of the classic Indian text). They all came with a 'warning' about the sexually explicit nature of the text. Or was that a recommendation?

In Menzies there are racks of erotic fiction, supposedly written by women, for women, but it's always men who seem to be browsing there. But even now, because they might be seen, they're frightened to buy. Shoplifting in that section is twenty times worse than in any other part of the shop. In a bid to stop it, the books have been put on a special shelf behind the counter.

You can buy uncensored sex videos in W. H. Smith now; since they are deemed educational. A curious aspect of British culture: the brandy is 'medicinal', the sex books are really 'manuals', the horny novels are 'adult literature', the porn videos are 'educational' – so long as it isn't entertainment, so long as we don't get any enjoyment, well, that's all right then.

High Street newsagents remain choosy about girlie mags, usually opting for the innocuous glamour of *Playboy* and *Penthouse*. Such finickety policy is disingenuously ascribed to sensitivity to customers, especially those with children. Yet half a dozen shelves along these same newsagents sell books about the vilest sex crimes and gung-ho garrotte thine enemy biographies, all in easy reach of any curious child. Even if such books are on the top shelf describing the minutest details of women raped and murdered seems OK, but simply boasting about a sexual encounter is deemed disgusting.

A couple of days after handing in the manuscript of *Blue Period* the doubts began. Was it wise to go so public? I kept thinking of all the ways in which the book could be misinterpreted, dreaded anyone calling it a half-hearted apologia for porn. I just wanted to tell the truth, be understood, absolved of guilt. But it was a huge risk. At the end of the day, what right had I really got to cast such serious aspersions on the whole of the UK's male population? Maybe it was just fiction, the flashers, the knicker-sniffers, the alfresco shaggers, no more than hearsay and saloon-bar jokes cobbled together by me into a pervy Domesday Book that had pretensions as some kind of social document. Habeas corpus, they'd cry. Let's see these men. Give us some names. But I couldn't. At the end of the day they were as hazy and apocryphal as figures on the grassy knoll.

On the evidence I'd penned, the only one who stood condemned was me.

Such were my doubts as I sat on the train between London and Derby. We'd just passed through Wellingborough station. As the train skirted a field, out from a straggling copse walked a man of about thirty, naked except for a short T-shirt. I blinked in disbelief. A real, live flasher. Not the kind who lurked in bushes waiting for a lone schoolgirl or a shopping pensioner – this man needed a whole trainload of witnesses, businesswomen, housewives and female students amongst them. Who was he? And what on earth would his mum/girlfriend/children think if they knew what he was up to? They probably never would. The flasher is always someone else, a bogeyman from the pages of the tabloids, a bespectacled old git in a grubby mac. Yet this one, fit and clean-shaven, looked as if he'd come hotfoot from the local gym.

The vision lasted only a few seconds, but it left me stunned. Boastful letters and muddy Polaroids had been a major part of my working life, but for all that it was all on paper – tall stories and jokes and women who were no more than coloured dots. None of it had ever seemed quite real. It wasn't fiction, exactly, but neither was it fact.

Years ago someone might have pulled the communication cord, but there was no obvious panic. One or two of my fellow passengers exchanged cautious smirks, but the rest preferred not to acknowledge the event at all. And so we travelled on, each one of us digesting its significance in our own way. Back in the dwindling distance the flasher still existed, hurriedly pulling his Y-fronts back on and skedaddling. Or, like a trainspotter, perhaps he sat in his car and had a smoke, calmly awaiting the next express, flashing in accordance with the British Rail timetable.

I mulled it over, tried to find a place for this bizarre event in my rambling narrative, grasping for import and significance. But why should I consider myself some kind of expert? Even after all those years on the front-line I have to admit that there is no easy answer, no ready-made slot to put this man in. Still, I settled back with a coffee (compliments of Midland Main Line) and felt a little easier about my story. Never mind the generalizations, I was right, wasn't I? There *was* something shadowy out there lurking in our fields and streets, a man with a lonesome prick and unknown intentions.

Acknowledgements

Blue Period wasn't an easy book to write. I laughed out loud on many occasions, but worried just as often about making some kind of serious contribution to an eternal debate. My thanks then to Ian Preece, my editor at Gollancz, for all his encouragement and suggestions and for keeping me on the right track. A mention in dispatches for Lucy, Mike, Hugo and everyone else who gave their support to the project, and especially Liz Knights, who commissioned it but sadly did not live to see it in the shops.